Pewter

Designs and Techniques

Pewter
Designs and Techniques

Fleur Grenier

THE CROWOOD PRESS

First published in 2010 by
The Crowood Press Ltd
Ramsbury, Marlborough
Wiltshire SN8 2HR

www.crowood.com

British Library Cataloguing-in-Publication Data
A catalogue record for this book is available from the British
Library.

ISBN 978 1 84797 158 6

Typeset by Servis Filmsetting Ltd, Stockport, Cheshire
Printed and bound in Malaysia by Konway Printhouse Sdn Bhd

FRONTISPIECE:
Blackened Chargers by Keith Tyssen

CONTENTS

INTRODUCTION

Pewter has been part of people's lives for many centuries. There is a long history and tradition associated with it. Many households today own a piece of pewter, whether it is a treasured family heirloom that has been passed from one generation to the next, a piece of tableware, a commemorative trophy or a tankard that was given for an eighteenth or twenty-first birthday present or even a Harry Potter ornament!

As well as being a traditional material it has also been at the forefront of fashionable trends for example during the Art Nouveau period, designer craftsmen Archibald Knox designed a collection for Liberty's of London using pewter. He produced elegant contemporary designs many of which survive today and became symbolic of the Art Nouveau Style.

Modern pewter is completely lead free. This means it does not tarnish or turn the dull grey colour of old pewter, which causes confusion for many people, as they do not expect pewter to be the shiny silver colour it is today. This is why people may not think they own a piece of pewter.

It has endless possibilities for different applications, so knowingly or unknowingly people may be using something made from pewter on a daily basis, or may have a pewter ornament of some kind.

Pewter is an inspiring material to work with. Its qualities lend itself to a variety of techniques and processes making it a very versatile metal to use. With all of the developments of technology today, pewtersmiths still use the traditional skills whether it is for a conventional or contemporary style of product. The exclusion of lead has meant that that health and safety issues are not a problem and the fact that it does not tarnish enables

OPPOSITE PAGE:
Glass and pewter desk tidy: cast glass and pewter tray, inkwell, blotter, paperknife and pen (made by the author for her final degree show while studying at The London Guildhall University).

Archibald Knox Jug (courtesy of The Worshipful Company of Pewterers).

pieces to retain a polished lustre finish that is more favourable for the fashionable contemporary styles of today.

I was first introduced to pewter while studying on the degree in Jewellery, Silversmithing and Allied Crafts at Sir John Cass, The London Metropolitan University in 1991. We were set a project using pewter, and this was a turning point for my work. I found pewter to be a lovely material to work with, and it was so versatile that it continually generated new ideas. Following this project I designed all the pieces for my degree show to be made with pewter. Each piece was made using a different skill and process, which was quite challenging as pewter is not a material that many people work with so there was some trial and error. Being taught silversmithing skills was a good grounding for my pewtersmithing as many of the techniques are the same; they just needed to be adapted to the pewter as it has different properties to precious and base metals.

Following my degree I was offered a place at The Royal College of Art on the Goldsmithing, Silversmithing, Metalwork and Jewellery course. This two-year MA course enabled me to push my design ideas further and improve my pewtersmithing skills, using them for more elaborate and complicated work. I wanted to use the pewter in a way that was not traditionally associated with it. This led to the creation of a range of bath-

Washbasin, tap soap dish and plug prototype; wash basin model made from Styrofoam sprayed with a plastic resin coating, author (Royal College of Art final show).

room accessories. My style is quite sculptural, but I also enjoy the challenge of creating a functional piece. Using drawings of the female form I developed them to create a soap dish and plug, tap, mirror and door handle, as well as a washbasin prototype to be made in ceramic. Since graduating from the RCA I have continued to work using pewter, designing and making contemporary designs that I sell through galleries, craft fairs and exhibitions, and I also teach.

Pewter is becoming increasingly popular whether it is as a hobby, a professional craftsperson or manufacturer. The aim of this book is not to explore the history of pewter, which has been well covered in other books. Rather I hope to demonstrate how pewter has developed into the material it is today, and how it has advanced and moved with trends and fashions through the years.

Throughout the book various techniques and processes are explored, with some step-by-step exercises to show techniques in an easy-to-follow format. Throughout there are examples of work by pewtersmiths from the UK and abroad, to demonstrate each procedure and show the range of items that can be made using each skill.

These exercises and examples are designed to give you a starting point. It is important to be able to move forward, make your own designs and develop your own skills. Do not be afraid to experiment. Making test pieces is always useful. It is a good idea to keep these test pieces together and attach a label, so that if you are referring to it at a future date you have a record of the process. Amazing work can be created from a small test piece or even from something that has come about accidentally.

All the techniques and processes described are from my own experience and that of several other pewtersmiths who have been kind enough to help by sharing skills in their field of expertise. As with a lot of skills, once you begin to work for yourself you may find variations on a specific process. This is the way most craftspeople develop. There is not always a right or wrong way; it is important to find the best way for you.

This book demonstrates how it is possible to work with pewter whether you are in a small workshop set up in a shed, a professional workshop, school or university. It sets out to create a record of what pewter is today – how it is being used by various designers, pewtersmiths and manufacturers, and the developments there have been in production techniques. Most importantly I hope it will inspire more designers and craftspeople to work with it, so pewter continues to be an inspiring material to work with and remains part of our lives for further centuries to come.

Desk clock with agate beads for the feet, author.

CHAPTER 1

WHAT IS PEWTER?

TIN   ANTIMONY   COPPER

Pewter is a malleable metal alloy, made predominately of tin. Tin in its natural state is very soft, so other elements, particularly antimony and copper, are added to make it more usable. Pewter was traditionally used to make domestic items such as cups and plates.

OPPOSITE PAGE:
Sculptural bowl by the author.

The pewter alloy constituents: tin, copper and antimony; pewter in its ready-made forms: pewter sheet, disc and ingot for casting.

The traditional image of pewter comes from pieces displaying a dull dark grey surface, indicating the presence of lead. Modern pewter, however, is completely lead free, and therefore is a shiny silver colour. Unlike silver and other metals pewter does not tarnish.

The percentage of tin is usually 92–98 per cent. The mix of the pewter alloy can vary depending on whether it will be used for casting or made into sheet. A typical casting mix will have a higher content of tin as the metal is usually not worked after casting, whereas sheet pewter will need the copper and antimony, as it will need to be to able to withstand the various processes it will be used for, such as hammering, stamping or spinning.

Up to 8 per cent of antimony is added, to increase the hardness. For processes such as spinning the percentage of antimony is kept below 5 per cent, to ensure it is soft enough. For casting the amount of antimony can be increased up to 8 per cent, as the castings are not usually worked on after they have been cast.

Copper, a maximum of 2.5 per cent, is added to give the metal durability, and it also binds the alloy together. When the alloy is melted antimony has a cuboid structure, and when the metal is heated these would float to the surface, but the copper has a needle star-like structure that captures the antimony and draws it into the tin, keeping an even distribution within the metal. If too much copper is added it can alter the colour of the pewter. If this copper-heavy mix is used for casting it can cause porosity, that is, pitted holes are present in the surface of the casting, which can ruin the finish of a piece.

Sometimes a very small amount of bismuth, cadmium or silver is also added for strength.

It is not unknown for some larger manufacturers to stipulate the quantities for the pewter alloy they use, as they have specific requirements for some of their products. These will however still be within the set guidelines of quantities, specified by the European standards.

How Pewter Is Made

The tin is melted in a large crucible up to around 450°C. The copper is added, then finally the antimony. It is mixed with a large paddle (stirrer), which ensures that the copper and antimony are thoroughly mixed with the tin. The temperature of the pewter is then reduced to around 317°C. If the metal is poured too quickly the tin and the antimony will not be mixed evenly in the metal and the pewter will have imperfections, some of which may not become apparent until the pewter is being used.

The pewter is then released from a hole at the base of the

Mixing crucible and moulds (courtesy of the Pewter Sheet Company, Birmingham).

crucible, so only the clean metal is being poured from below the surface where the dross (oxidized layer on the surface of the pewter when molten) will have formed. If the dross was poured into the moulds it would make imperfections in the pewter. For casting the pewter is poured into iron moulds to make smaller ingots. In its cast state the pewter is harder than in any other form.

For sheets, it is poured into larger rectangular slab moulds which are eventually rolled into sheets. The large slabs of pewter are fed through large rollers to make sheet. It is important that these rollers have a smooth polished finish as any marks, indents or pieces of dirt will transfer onto the pewter as it is passed through. To prepare the slabs for the rollers they need to be machined on the top and bottom to create a smooth surface.

The pewter is rolled in one direction, then turned and repeated in another direction; this is particularly important

Stirring the pewter mix
(courtesy of the Pewter Sheet
Company, Birmingham).

Pouring the metal into
the slaps ready for rolling
(courtesy of the Pewter Sheet
Company, Birmingham).

if the pewter is being used for a process such as spinning. When the pewter is being rolled the metal's structure is being changed. As it is rolled and compressed the metal becomes softer than in its pure cast state, because the crystals break down. If the pewter was rolled in only one direction and was then used for spinning, the metal would have an uneven strength and when moved against the former sections it would move quicker than others, making it difficult to control completely.

One of the many advantages of working with pewter is that it can be recycled. Any scrap or failed castings can simply be remelted, which means there is never any waste.

The History

Pewter was introduced into Britain by the Romans around the third century AD, but it was not until around the thirteenth century however that large-scale production began, predominately with ecclesiastical items. By the fourteenth century almost every market town had a pewterer in its craft guild.

Being a pewterer had become an important trade, and pewterers had a high standing within their community. To maintain this standard a group of London pewterers formed a guild which controlled the quality of the pewter and the items produced. The first reference to this guild was in 1348, when they asked the Mayor and Corporation of London for control over the composition of the pewter alloy being used.

In 1474 Edward IV granted the guild its first Royal Charter, which then enabled them to have legal control over the pewter industry throughout England. After this the guild became known as The Worshipful Company of Pewterers. The charter gave the Company power to confiscate substandard pewter. Officers were sent throughout Britain to carry out inspections using an assay mould, which was filled with the

Touchmark plate (courtesy of The Worshipful Company of Pewterers).

THE TOUCHMARK

**Touchmarks
(courtesy of A.R. Wentworth (Sheffield) Ltd).**

Traditionally, all pewterers were required to mark their work with a stamp known as a 'strike', similar to the stamp used by a silversmith. This was introduced by act of Parliament in 1503. As the silversmith's stamp is registered with the assay office the pewtersmith's mark had to be registered with The Worshipful Company of Pewterers. This registration was done by using their strike on a touchplate, which was kept as a record by the Company so that work could be identified, and if not made to the correct standard the pewtersmith could be notified and the work withdrawn.

At first registration was used solely for hollowware – items such as drinking vessels salt and pepper pots – but from 1522 this was extended to all items made in pewter. It is not known whether similar plates were used outside London as none have been found, but a plate has survived showing the marks of Scottish pewterers.

At its peak so much pewter was used that seventeenth century diarist Samuel Pepys wrote after the Great Fire of London in 1666, 'The streets were flowing with molten metal.' Most of the touchplates were destroyed by the Great Fire, and all the London pewterers were called to restrike their mark. Five of the touchplates dating from 1668 have survived and are kept at the Worshipful Company of Pewterers' Hall.

The touchmark ceremony is still performed at the hall, and pewterers are able to register their mark. While originally registration served to check standards of pewter, today it is more commonly used as a means of keeping a record of pewter so future generations can identify the pieces and find out more about the maker.

Today makers and manufacturers use their own mark. In addition to this there are three other common marks: that of the Association of British Pewter Craftsmen (ABPC), found on items made by ABPC members; the Seahorse, used to identify pewter of fine quality; and the European Pewter Union (EPU) used by members of the EPU.

Archibald Knox Plate (courtesy of The Worshipful Company of Pewterers).

pewter being used by the pewtersmith and then weighed. If the casting removed from the mould was heavier than the standard casting, this indicated the presence of too much lead.

In about 1650, Huguenot James Taudin produced a new alloy 'hard metal,' with the lead removed, and composed of predominantly tin with a small amount of copper, antimony and bismuth. The antimony increased the hardness of the metal and produced a mirror-like finish when polished. Initially The Worshipful Company of Pewterers did not approve of the new alloy, but Taudin had strong allies – Oliver Cromwell and King Charles II – and after the King wrote a fierce letter to the Company, the objections were overruled.

By the seventeenth century practically every household in Britain owned and used pewterware products on a daily basis – items such as plates, tankards, candlesticks, buttons, bowls and many other everyday items. This new metal was more practical than the plates and utensils made of wood and horn. Pewter was durable and elegant, and was no longer the metal just for nobility.

Following this period of popularity strong competition was introduced from cheap mass-produced crockery made of glass, porcelain and alternative metals such brass and steel. These all assisted in the slow decline of pewter production.

With the arrival of the Arts and Crafts Movement in the early twentieth century artisans started to rebel against the new industrialized world. With this movement pewter again regained its popularity. Liberty's of London commissioned renowned designers of the time, Archibald Knox and Rex Silver, to develop a collection of pewter which became very popular and is highly sought after today. This again raised the profile of pewter, making it the metal of the time.

Although pewter has never regained the huge popularity it had in the seventeenth century it has always been a part of people's lives. Over the centuries the pewter craftspeople and manufacturers have demonstrated their ability to adapt.

In 1970 the Association of British Pewter Craftsmen (ABPC) was initiated by The Worshipful Company of Pewterers. The ABPC works on behalf of the individual pewterers and manufacturers to ensure that the standard of pewter is maintained, for example by drawing attention to items sold as pewter which in fact are not. They also work actively to promote pewter, to continuously raise its profile.

The Worshipful Company Pewterers is one of the few livery companies that are still connected with all aspects of their trade. Their hall in London is home to a priceless collection of documents and pieces that tell the long story of pewter and its influence and impact on people's lives.

CHAPTER 2

WORK AREA AND BASIC WORKING TECHNIQUES

WORK AREA

One of the advantages of working with pewter is that you can start working with a relatively small amount of equipment. This is obviously dependent upon the type of work you will be doing. Throughout this book various techniques and processes will be described, each depicting relevant equipment that will be needed for a specific process.

Workshop Layout

When setting up your workshop it is important to plan the layout. For the majority of pewtersmithing processes used there are three basic areas that will need to be considered.

MAIN BENCH

To start with a bench is a priority. A jeweller's bench is advisable: this is a hard wood construction with a semicircle cut out of the front, a design which enables the craftsperson to set up the area with tools regularly needed, so that pliers and cutters are within easy reach. A wedge is inserted in the middle of the semi-circle; this acts as a support for the work while filing and sawing.

This bench is built to a height of 81–98cm, so you can work sitting down; this ensures that if you are working at your bench for long periods of time you do not suffer from back problems, as good posture is maintained. A comfortable chair is also important for when you are working for long periods of time.

OPPOSITE PAGE:
Jeweller's bench.

It is possible to build a bench. It should be strong and secure, so there is no movement while working. A hardwood top will give the bench strength and durability and ensure the bench will last. It is also possible to buy a clamp to secure a wedge to the bench. This can be useful if the bench has to be used for a variety of applications, in which case it may need to be removed.

The position of the bench is important for good visibility. If it can be placed near natural light this will help reduce eyestrain; a lamp with a daylight bulb is also a good idea. Be aware of the direction of the sun coming in through a window; sometimes being directly in sunlight can be a problem.

General working bench with pillar drill, vice, steel plate, hollow formers and punches.

GENERAL BENCH

A separate bench for doing shaping, forming and general work is also recommended. An ideal height for this general bench is to be waist height, so it is suitable for doing work while standing. Again hardwood is an ideal material.

This area can be used to fit a pillar drill and a vice. Small pillar drills can be bought relatively cheaply from most tool shops and can be a useful piece of equipment. Ensure you follow safety guidelines when using a pillar drill. It is a good idea to practise drilling on a scrap piece of pewter. As it is softer than most metals, very little pressure is needed to make a hole.

The size of the vice is really dependent on the type of work you will be doing; if working on a small scale a small vice will be adequate. When fitting a vice make sure the jaw is positioned so it overhangs the front of the bench, so when you are working with larger or longer pieces the piece can hang below the bench. If it can be placed at the end of the bench it is preferable, but this is not always feasible. Ensure sure there is room for you to move around, as if you are using stakes to form pieces you will need to have space to hammer.

Small pillar drills can be bought relatively cheaply from most tool shops and can be a useful piece of equipment. Ensure that you follow safety guidelines when using a pillar drill. Always wear safety glasses. Before using it familiarize yourself with the controls, most importantly on and off, but also how to insert the drill bits and move the table up and down. It is also a good idea to practise drilling on a scrap piece of pewter.

SOLDERING AREA

The general working bench can also be used for soldering, but if you do have room for a separate area this is more suitable. It is better to set up a soldering area away from direct sunlight, as it is easier to see the flame on your torch and the soldered joint, if it is not too light.

Although not essential, a turntable is helpful for soldering – one that is used for ceramics will be fine, or you can use a metal working turntable; this will have a firebrick set into it whereas a ceramic working turntable will just have a steel top. The turntable enables you to set up the object to be soldered, then move it round freely, without handling the piece. This is particularly useful when soldering larger areas as you can turn the table so the torch can be moved along the seam in one movement, which draws the solder along the joint, creating an even soldered joint.

You will also need flat firebrick sheets, which come in various sizes. It is good to have some blocks as they can be useful to support to work while it is being soldered or to hold the ladle in position when the pewter is being melted for casting. These blocks also come in numerous sizes. You will also need a torch (details of which will be discussed further in the soldering section), tweezers, flux and solder.

Vice.

Hand Tools

These are the most regularly used hand tools:

Pliers: Flat nose wide or snipe nose parallel, half round, round nose, flat and tin snips.

Hammers: Rawhide mallet, wooden bossing mallet, and ball pein hammer. Wooden mallets and stakes are always preferable when working with the pewter. As it is such a soft material, metal hammers and formers mark the work a lot more, and it will take longer to remove them and finish the piece.

Saws: Jeweller's piercing saw and blades. The jeweller's saw is one of the most useful pieces of equipment for general cutting.

Files: Half round, flat and oval files are useful; a mix of second cut and smooth cut will probably be used the most. Coarser files leave more marks in the pewter and are harder to

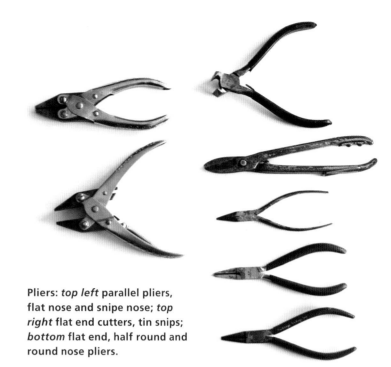

Pliers: *top left* parallel pliers, flat nose and snipe nose; *top right* flat end cutters, tin snips; *bottom* flat end, half round and round nose pliers.

Selection of rawhide, bossing and rubber mallets.

Jeweller's saws: *right to left* normal frame, adjustable frame and deep throat saw.

RIGHT: **Selection of files, emery stick and wire brush for cleaning files.**

remove. A set of needle files is needed for detail filing. (As the pewter is soft it clogs the files quite quickly, so it is useful to have a steel brush that can be used to clean them.) Never use a file without a handle as this can cause serious injury if you slip while using it.

Emery stick: the emery sticks you can buy come with a single sheet of emery paper glued directly onto the wood; these are preferable for jewellery. With larger scale work, however, where more paper is likely to be used it is better to make your own. Take a sheet of emery paper and tightly fold it around the stick (which can be rectangular, round or half round), using masking tape to secure the tape at both ends onto the stick. You can use it to emery your piece and then, once that face of the emery stick is no longer of use, it can be torn off revealing a fresh piece of emery beneath. Various shapes and sizes can be made depending on the type of piece you are working on. 400 grit is a good general grade of paper, with 220 when a coarser grade is needed or 600 for finer.

WORKING WITH PRECIOUS METALS

If the workshop is used for pieces made in precious metals such as silver and gold, a separate area for working in pewter is advisable, if you have the space. This is due to pewter contamination: if a tiny bit of pewter dust comes into contact with silver or gold and it is then heated, the pewter will eat through the precious metal creating a hole; the more it is heated the larger the hole will become.

It is possible to use pewter in the same workshop as precious metals; it is just important to be sensible. Have a separate set of files, saw blades and steel brush. Do not use emery paper or polishing mops that have been used with pewter, as these are all tools which will retain some pewter. Stakes, pliers, drill bits and hammers can be shared as long as the surfaces are cleaned with a very fine wire wool when you have finished. It

is also a good idea not to just sweep down any benches but to use a vacuum cleaner, as this will remove the finer dust.

This is the basic equipment and tools needed. Further equipment can be bought as you progress with your work and you learn which techniques you are going to develop and become aware of the equipment you will need.

BASIC WORKING TECHNIQUES

Cutting

JEWELLER'S PIERCING SAW

The jeweller's saw is one of the most useful pieces of equipment; it can be used for general piercing or to cut very intricate detailed work. The saw can be used to cut precious and non-precious metal, but it can also be used to cut softer materials such as shell, Styrofoam and wood. It is also possible to buy spiral teeth blades that are ideal for cutting wax, rubber and Perspex, as the blades do not become clogged. The frames vary in depth from 5cm to the deep throat saws which are 20cm. The deeper frames are useful for cutting larger sheets of metal; however they can be more difficult to use and control for general piercing. Adjustable frames are

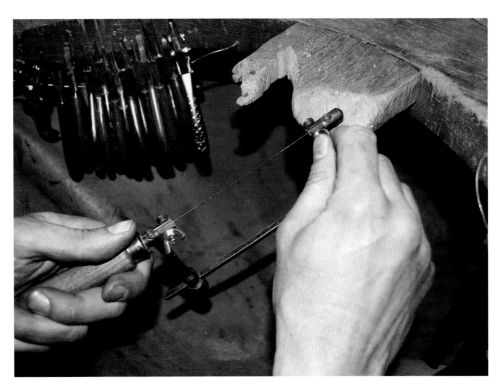

Fitting a blade into a jeweller's saw.

also available to allow for different lengths of blade or for broken blades to be used.

When choosing blades to work with be sure to choose the correct size blades; the blades are very fragile and it is inevitable that some will break. Experience using the saw and using the right size blade will help to reduce the number of breakages. The blades come in various sizes, 8/0 being the finest through to 0, then increasing to 14; the standard sizes available from most suppliers is 8/0 to 5.

On a spiral blade the teeth spiral down the blade, which allows the saw to cut in any direction. Spiral blades can be used to cut metal as well as softer materials and can be more practical for materials that will constantly clog the saw, such as wax. They are available in more limited sizes ranging from 5 to 2/0.

For cutting thinner sheets of metal, finer blades are used; if the blade is too coarse it will catch on the metal, making it very difficult to cut. For most of the general piercing a 0 or 1 size blade will be suitable; for cutting off sprues on casting and thicker material, courser blades should be used.

To fit a blade into the frame, undo the nuts at either end of the frame. Hold the blade with the teeth facing upwards and sloping down towards the handle (if you run your finger gently over the blade it will feel smoother when your finger runs from the far side of the frame towards your body – do not use too much pressure or it will cut your finger). Insert one end fully between the nut and frame, then tighten the screw.

When putting in a blade make sure there is tension in the blade; if it is too loose it will catch on the metal and break. As it is difficult to create the tension needed to insert the opposite end with just your hands, a more practical way is to position the handle of the saw towards your hip and lean the end of the frame into the bench; by leaning into the frame this pushes the two ends in. If you then secure the blade between the nut and frame at the opposite end of the saw and tighten it, this should create the tension needed. If you then test the blade for tension it should make a high-pitched sound.

The saw needs very little effort to cut through the metal; you should only really be guiding it rather than forcing it along the line you are following. Position your metal on the bench peg and with your saw vertical to the metal slowly move the saw up and down letting the saw do the work. Use the full length of the blade. If you find it catches on the metal, run beeswax over the surface of the blade to give a smoother movement.

If you need to make sharp turns or corners, do not just turn the blade as this will cause it to snap. Move the blade slowly

Guillotine, with combined sheet metal bender, roller and guillotine (Axminster tools).

up and down on the spot, slowly rotating the frame until the blade is pointing the direction you want to go and then continue. It is inevitable that blades will be broken as they are quite fragile; this will however reduce once you become more experienced with the saw.

GUILLOTINE/SHEARS

On a large scale in a more commercial environment, large foot operated or power operated machines are used. However for a smaller workshop small hand-operated guillotines can be bought. Many of the hand-operated machine also have facilities for bending and rolling the metal. They are relatively inexpensive and can be useful, although not essential, for a small-scale workshop.

The guillotine is designed to cut straight sections of metal accurately. When you pull the arm down it firstly brings down a plate to grip the metal to be cut; then an angled blade is forced down and slices the metal along the length, shearing it off cleanly. A sharp burr will be made on the edge of the metal, but this can be removed with a file and then it is ready to use.

BAND SAW/SCROLL SAW

Both these are ideal for cutting larger pieces of pewter. They are a lot coarser than a jeweller's saw, and the edges will need

Scrollsaw.

to be filed and emeryed more in order to remove the saw marks and sharp burrs on the edge. You must also allow for the fact that the blade itself is thicker than a jeweller's saw so there will be more material to cut away. If using a scroll saw, buy blades with smaller teeth designed to be used on metal. There is more scope for creating curves on a scroll saw – not very tight ones but more than can be achieved with a band saw.

OTHER METHODS OF CUTTING

To cut small areas tin snips are ideal. For thin sheet pewter a Stanley knife with a steel rule can be used. Extreme care should be used when working with a Stanley knife, as they are so sharp. For very thin sheet such as the sheet used for *Repoussé* work it is even possible to cut with a craft knife or pair of sharp scissors.

Soldering

To solder pewter you use the same principles as soldering other metals, either precious or base metals. The joint must always be clean and neatly fitting together. A flux is used to assist the solder in flow and to clean the joint.

As with other metals it is important to use the correct solder and flux for pewter. The main difference when soldering

pewter is that pewter has a much lower melting point than other metals, starting to melt at 240°C. This means that when soldering care must be taken not to melt the piece. A small butane hand torch is ideal.

EQUIPMENT

Turntable: Revolving table to enable the piece that is being soldered to be rotated, thus allowing the solder to flow freely, creating an even soldered joint.

- Steel tweezers
- Fire resistant sheet and blocks (as discussed above)

FLUX

Flux is very important for the soldering process. Without flux the solder will melt but it will stay in a lump on the surface and not neatly flow around the joint. The flux creates a capillary reaction so the solder flows more easily.

It is possible to make a flux. The most commonly used mix is one part hydrochloric acid and nine parts glycerine; however it is not always practical to mix your own. Many commercial companies mix their own for their specific products and solder used. A lot of the off-the-shelf fluxes for lead-free soldering are suitable, for example: Frys, Powerflo Flux paste. Care should be taken to avoid fluxes that are too corrosive, such as Baker's fluid, as they will mark the surface of the pewter.

Soldering set-up: turntable, fire resistant sheet, torch, tweezers, firebricks, solder and flux.

SOLDER

As with silver or gold soldering there are various types of solders available. A general solder for sheet work is the tin and bismuth mix, a lower melting point solder being 70 per cent tin and 30 per cent bismuth, with a slightly higher mix being 45 per cent tin 55 per cent bismuth. Solders are produced in thin spaghetti length and width strips and are quite brittle due to the bismuth content. It is also possible to use a pure tin wire, more suitable for heavier gauge metal, or thin strips of pewter creating a welded joint.

BUTANE HAND-HELD TORCH

As a very small amount of heat is needed, this torch is suitable for all work that needs to be soldered, whether large or small. Unlike other metals where the whole piece must be heated for the solder to flow neatly around the joint, with pewter the torch is focused solely on the area you are soldering, as too much heat will simply melt the piece of work.

A very soft gentle flame is all that is needed. The lowest setting on the torch is ample for sheet work, and it may need to be increased slightly for soldering thicker gauge sheet and castings. The torch should not be held in one position, as this will create too much heat; it should be drawn gently backwards and forwards on the area to be soldered. Remember that the hottest point on the flame is at the tip of the pale blue part of the flame. It is preferable if the area where you are soldering is not too well lit so you are able to see the flame and the solder as it flows.

THE SOLDERING PROCESS

Before starting to solder place a fire-resistant sheet on the turntable and set up your work in position for soldering. It is good to get into the habit of brushing down the fire-resistant sheet after you have used it, as any bits of solder that are left on it could melt onto another piece when it is heated on the sheet. The aim is to be able to produce a clean neat joint that has no lumps of solder and will therefore need little work done on it to clean it up.

It is better to practise the various techniques on some scrap pewter before moving onto a proper piece, as you need to acquire the skill to control the flame without melting the object. Even an experienced metal worker must become familiar with the metal and its characteristics which will differ from other metals that they have worked with.

First make sure the joints are clean and they fit tightly together and the solder is clean (if it has been left out on the bench for a while an oxide will appear on the surface which will hinder the soldering process, so this should be removed with either a wire wool or fine emery).

Brush flux along the joint. Apply it carefully as the solder

Soldering with paillons.

Stick soldering.

will flow into it, and a misplaced piece of solder will follow the flux and run over the surface creating more cleaning up at the end. Do not apply too much: pools of flux can also hinder the solder flowing, as it has to heat itself in order for the solder to melt.

There are two methods of applying the solder: with small pellets of solder known as paillons or with stick solder. Paillons are positioned along the seam, or solder can be stick fed into the joint; this takes a bit more practice but once successfully achieved can create a very neat joint.

Paillon soldering: Using a small pair of wire cutters cut small pellets of solder approximately 1mm. Using tweezers or a brush position them about 1.5cm apart around the joint to be soldered. Gently start to heat the area, making sure both pieces of pewter that you want to solder together are heated equally. The solder will naturally flow to the piece that is the hottest.

Keep the torch moving until the solder starts to melt. As it starts to melt move the torch along the joint; this will draw the solder along creating an even seam. If you find one of the pellets is not melting straight away continue to move the torch onto the next piece, turning the table. Solder attracts solder, so as you move round the solder pellets are all drawn into each other producing an even soldered joint. If a piece falls off while soldering you can replace it, but rather than letting the metal cool down completely while you look for it, if you cannot see it straightaway then use a new piece and continue soldering.

Stick soldering: If using a stick solder, prepare the metal in the same way except do not cut the solder. Heat the metal gently. When the flux starts to bubble touch the end of the seam with the stick of solder. Be careful not to feed the solder directly into the flame as the solder will melt before it touches the metal; this will cause the solder to melt and drip, not necessarily onto the seam. Turn the table so the solder follows the flame around the joint, adding more solder as necessary.

Care should be taken when considering which angle the torch is held at. It must be suitable for both pieces to receive equal heat so the solder does not just flow on one half. Watch to see that the flame is not deflecting on to another area of the piece, as it may look like all the heat is on one point but suddenly a different area will start to melt.

If you are soldering two pieces of sheet together, gently move the flame equally between the two. If you are soldering a small piece onto a larger section or a casting, however, the casting is likely to be heavier. This means that the casting will have to be heated more to bring it to the same temperature as the sheet. Gently heat the heavier pewter to raise the temperature, and then move the flame across so the smaller piece is also heated. The solder should start to flow equally along the joint between the two pieces.

Once the piece has been soldered leave it to cool. Do not move it too quickly, as some heat is retained in the piece, particularly larger pieces, which can mean the solder is still at a pasty stage and if moved it will either break off completely or become a weak joint.

Heating the solder and removing with the side of the steel tweezers.

Commercial soldering, A.R. Wentworth (Sheffield) Ltd.

When it has cooled wash the piece with soapy water to remove the flux, so the flux does not get transferred onto the polishing mops.

If an error has been made, reflux the joint. Gently reheat the joint and remove with either a pair of tweezers or with a gloved hand. As the pewter is a poor conductor of heat the heat will not transfer to the rest of the piece quickly.

If soldering more complicated shapes, use firebricks to keep the piece in position. Binding wire can also be used, and on some occasions it is possible to hold the piece in position with your hands. If using this method wear gloves to stop any risk of being burned; a thick cotton glove will be sufficient for the heat not to come through to your hands.

Commercial manufacturers have their torch secured to a bench and then hold the piece together with their hands while gently moving it under the static flame. This gives them more control positioning the piece and over the flame.

The heat does not discolour the pewter, as it does some other metals. This means that some of the polishing of the piece can be done prior to soldering, which is ideal if once the piece is assembled there are some areas that will be difficult to get into with the polishing mop. It is advisable to do the first stage of polishing (see Chapter 6) before soldering. Once the piece has been polished the area to be soldered should be cleaned of any grease left by the polishing compound used; this can be done with a fine emery 600 grade or fine wire wool.

After the soldering is complete the only mark left is from the flux. This usually looks like a watermark on the surface but can be removed when doing the final stage of polishing. If any solder has gone outside the joint this will need to be removed; if it is on the surface try not to make too many deep marks with files as this will create a lot more work when it comes to finishing the piece. If it is a lump of solder on the surface and it is near to the edge of the piece, it is sometimes better to gently heat the solder, then when it has become liquid using the side of a pair of steel tweezers scrape the excess solder away and off the piece. It can then usually be cleaned with just emery paper rather than having to use files as well.

As with other metals there are different grades of solder made for specific jobs and many suppliers have their own mixes. The higher melting solders have a high content of tin; this obviously makes the soldering temperature quite close to the melting point of the pewter, and some of the lower melting lead-free solders can be quite brittle due to the bismuth content, so it is worth experimenting with different types to get a feel for which will work better on the pieces you are working on.

For a completely seam-free joint it is possible to fuse the seam together using pewter. This method can only really be used when two thicker pieces of pewter are being soldered together. When preparing the two halves file the edges at a slight angle so a v-shape is created. Cut a thin strip of pewter, flux the two halves and lay the strip onto the joint. Use a sharper, more intense flame to get the immediate area to fuse together.

The three sections fuse together like a welded joint, leaving a raised seam. The raised seam is then filed and emeryed ready for polishing. The advantage of this method is that as pewter is being fused to pewter, once it has been polished there will be no sign of a visible joint. This method can also be used to repair a piece if a hole has been melted into it accidentally. Simply flux the hole and plug it with a small piece of pewter which when pushed into the hole is slightly raised above the surface. Heat it until the plug has completely melted into the piece.

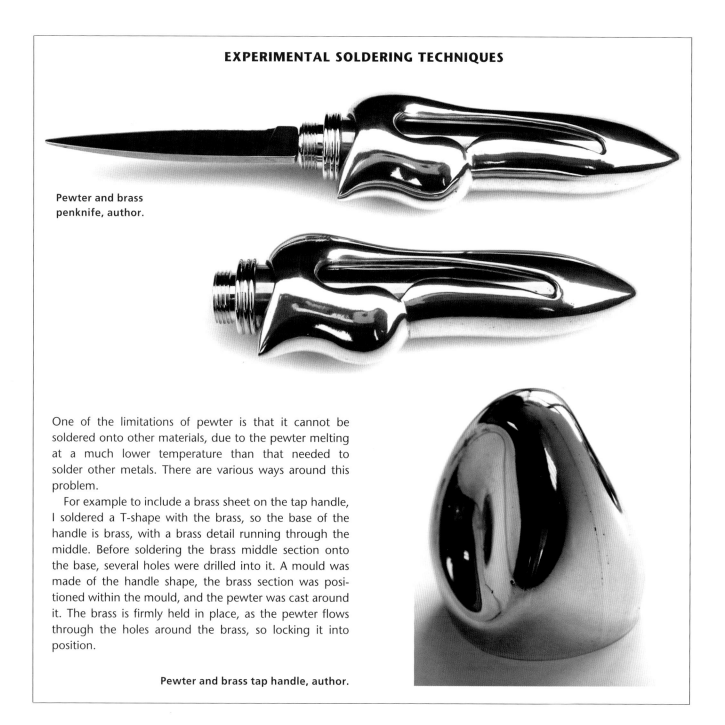

EXPERIMENTAL SOLDERING TECHNIQUES

**Pewter and brass
penknife, author.**

One of the limitations of pewter is that it cannot be soldered onto other materials, due to the pewter melting at a much lower temperature than that needed to solder other metals. There are various ways around this problem.

For example to include a brass sheet on the tap handle, I soldered a T-shape with the brass, so the base of the handle is brass, with a brass detail running through the middle. Before soldering the brass middle section onto the base, several holes were drilled into it. A mould was made of the handle shape, the brass section was positioned within the mould, and the pewter was cast around it. The brass is firmly held in place, as the pewter flows through the holes around the brass, so locking it into position.

Pewter and brass tap handle, author.

To include a pewter detail as shown in the pewter and copper pendant, I used a variation of this technique. The main section of the pendant was constructed in copper. The pewter was poured into the frame, then the rough surface was emeryed flat, to show the copper detail that has the appearance of an inlay.

An alternative method can be used with a pure tin paste. This is especially useful when working with a large item, which needs the main frame to be made from a material that has more strength than pewter.

For example the main structural branches of the Rainforest Light were made from brass rod, while all the mushroom heads were cast in pewter. My idea was to give the piece the overall look of pewter, with the branches appearing to have droplets of water on them.

When pure tin paste is brushed onto the surface, then gently heated with a large torch, the paste forms into little

Copper with inlayed pewter pendant, Julian Wolchover.

Rainforest Light: base frame MDF covered with beaten pewter foil that has been blackened, with carved American walnut on top; branches brass coated with tin paste and mushroom heads cast pewter, author (photographer Steve Speller).

Rainforest Light detail, showing tin paste (photographer Steve Speller).

droplets of tin. Care must be taken not to overheat the paste, or the droplet effect will be lost and it will look more like smooth plating over the surface.

An advantage of this tin paste coating is that the paste adheres to the surface of the brass and this then creates a material that the pewter can be soldered onto, commonly known as tinning. Using a low melting solder the joint was fluxed and the mushrooms soldered onto the stems. The paste has a flux in it, which has to be washed and thoroughly removed.

Since the brass has not been completely covered in paste, where the brass is exposed to the air the bright finish is lost and the dull tarnish then compliments the design.

CHAPTER 3

CASTING

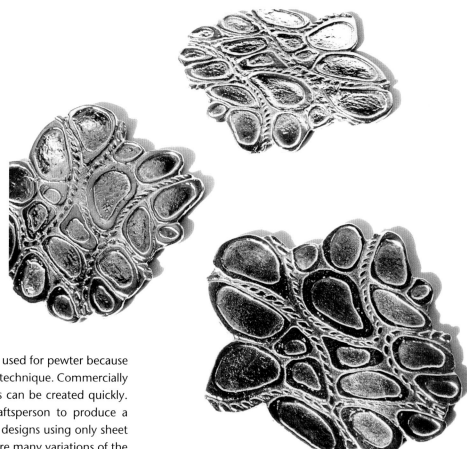

Cast coasters, author.

Casting is one of the main processes used for pewter because its properties are ideally suited to the technique. Commercially it is used because identical multiples can be created quickly. On a smaller scale it enables a craftsperson to produce a wide variety of work. While creating designs using only sheet pewter can be quite limiting, there are many variations of the casting and mould making process so designs do not usually have to be compromised.

For someone just starting out it can be inexpensive to set up, as it can be done with very little equipment and results can be achieved very quickly.

OPPOSITE PAGE:
Molten pewter.

Casting also has the advantage that any mistakes, sprues or off-cuts can be re-used by simply melting them again, which means there is no waste. Sometimes producing a design using other methods can create a lot of waste material, whereas casting uses only the required amount of material.

There are two casting methods: gravity casting and

centrifugal casting. Here we will concentrate on the gravity casting as this is more suited to a smaller scale workshop or someone just starting to use pewter. If you do become more involved in pewter you may decide the centrifugal casting machine would be a useful piece of equipment. The commercial pewter you see for sale in a shop is generally produced by centrifugal casting.

There are several processes to be followed before you have a complete casting. Initially you need a pattern, the object you want to recreate in pewter. The pattern can be made from a variety of materials as will be discussed. It is essential that the pattern is of a high standard of finish, as every item that is cast using this pattern will be exactly the same. If the finish is not perfect or a hole is not quite the right size, each casting produced from it will have to be corrected, so it is worth spending time making sure the pattern is just right.

Next comes the mould. This is the tool you pour the pewter into. Again there are a number of materials and ways to produce the mould, many of which will be discussed. Like the pattern it needs to be just right, as molten metal will be poured into it and this will produce the final piece.

The last stage is casting the molten metal. Techniques and safety issues will be covered here so pieces can be safely and confidently cast in pewter.

Basic Equipment

Melting pot: To melt the pewter, when first starting it is possible to use a torch with a large nozzle and a ladle. The only disadvantage is that it is not so easy to control the temperature, but there are thermometers available to buy for this purpose. If you decide to work more with pewter casting it is recommended that you buy a melting pot. These have a cast iron lining and have an inbuilt thermometer to control the temperature. They vary in size from 5kg, then increasing in size to hold much larger quantities for commercial producers. If you know you will be working on small-scale pieces a 5kg pot would be fine, but this only fits the small ladle. If you do not want to be limited to smaller work the 20kg pot would be more useful. The advantage of having an electric melting pot is that the pewter remains molten, so it will not need to be remelted between each casting, and the temperature can easily be controlled. When casting intricate detailed pieces the temperature can be raised so the molten metal flows around the mould without cooling too quickly. The increased temperature enables the pewter to flow through the whole mould keeping intricate details and sharp lines.

Powder: Graphite powder, French chalk or talc is used to help the pewter flow freely around the mould, create

Melting pewter using a ladle supported with firebricks and heated with a blowtorch.

Casting set-up: melting pot, ladle, scraper to remove dross, tin to collect dross, long arm leather gloves, large tray to hold mould, graphite powder, French chalk, brush, clamps, long nose pliers and mould.

a smooth surface and help the casting to release from the mould. It can be contained in something as simple as a sock tied at the top to make a bag, which can then be gently tapped on the surface of the moulds or it can be brushed on.

Ladle: If using a ladle to melt the pewter in, they are available in various sizes and the larger size is preferable. Cast iron ladles are better for hand casting as they retain the heat for longer, so the metal keeps its temperature.

Metal tray: Moulds are set up in a tray ready for casting, and the tray keeps the molten metal contained. A basic baking tray can be used.

G-Clamps: Clamps are used to hold the moulds together while pouring in the pewter. One or two clamps will be needed, depending on the size of the mould being used.

Dusting Brush: A soft paintbrush or old make-up brush is used to brush the excess talc or graphite powder from the mould.

Firebricks and sheets: If heating the pewter in a ladle the firebricks can be placed around the ladle, to support it and to help retain the heat.

Pliers: Large snipe nose pliers are used to remove the casting from the mould if it is still warm.

Wire: Binding wire is used to hold the two halves together securely while pouring in the metal, usually for the cuttlefish casting.

Pattern

The pattern is any object that is used to take a mould from. You may already have a design which you would like to create multiples from, or you can of course make your own pattern.

Selection of patterns made in wood, plaster, blue wax and metal.

There are very few limits on the type of material that may be used, except in cases where the mould relies on any heat treatment to assist in the curing process to solidify the rubber, which will not be discussed here. When choosing your pattern consideration should be given to the type of mould that you will use. For example if the pattern has an undercut, a protruding or concave feature that can hinder the withdrawal of the cast from the mould, then it would not be suitable for a rigid plaster mould, but a flexible silicone mould could be used.

Materials

NATURAL ORGANIC FORMS
These might include shells, twigs, bones and seeds.

METAL
Many metals can be used for patterns, for example brass, silver, copper, nickel, aluminium, steel, gilding metal or bronze. You may already have an object in mind or you can make something using other metalworking processes such as soldering, casting, shaping or forming.

WAX
There are many waxes available for sculpting with. One of the most practical is Blue carving wax, a synthetic wax that is very hard and can be machined, carved, sawed, drilled, turned on a lathe or used on CNC mills. With wax it is possible to get a very smooth finish close to that of metal, and it is quite often used by jewellers for prototypes of pieces of jewellery.

To work with the wax by hand there are various stages. First, to roughly cut shapes you can use a wood coping saw or a jeweller's saw. Jewellery blades can be used for thin small sections, but as they become clogged very easily it is better to use wax saw blades. On a wax blade the teeth spiral down the blade to stop it from becoming clogged with the wax. These also come in various sizes.

When working on larger pieces, sometimes the wax blocks purchased are too small. The wax can be melted and poured into a mould that is large enough to carve the design. As the wax contains polyester it melts at a higher temperature than some other waxes, so this should be taken into consideration when deciding what to pour the mould into. It will melt at approximately 108°C, It should be noted that when wax melts it does lose some of its properties; although it will be reusable for general carving and working it will not have the same strength if you want to machine it after it has been melted. There is a lot of shrinkage, particularly if the piece is large and deep, so be sure to allow for this. The wax can also crack if you are trying to make quite thick blocks.

When the wax has completely cooled it can be carved. Large rasp files can be used to take away the majority of the wax. For working on smaller pieces you can also buy small rasp and wax files. If you want to add small sections of wax, or repair cracks, a soldering iron can be used. It is useful to keep one separate for use solely on the wax so it does not pick up other materials.

Once you have the shape you can emery it with a coarse sandpaper to remove any rough rasp and file marks, then work through the different sandpapers until finishing on 400 wet and dry paper, keeping it wet to stop a build-up of the wax.

When the whole piece is complete, use a soft cloth to rub white spirit over the surface. This creates a reaction with the wax and dissolves the surface, causing it to break down into a paste. Rubbing this thoroughly with a soft cloth creates a smooth polished finish on the wax that is perfect for making a mould from.

PLASTER BLOCK
Make a plaster block and leave to dry completely. Once dried you can carve plaster with files, rasps, wax carving tools and then finish with a fine emery, 400 grade. To create a smooth polished finish on the plaster, use a wax release agent (a thick wax having the consistency of beeswax) rubbed onto the surface, then left for a few minutes to dry, it goes hard. You can then rub it with a soft cloth to buff the plaster, creating a smooth surface to make the mould from. Using the wax release also enables you to cast a plaster pattern in a plaster mould and remove it easily.

MILLIPUT
Working with Milliput is like using clay or Plasticine. You can shape it to the shape you require. A lot of work can be done while it is soft, but it can also be worked on when it is hard. Milliput is a compound that comes in two-parts, a hardener and a resin. Mixing the two parts together triggers a reaction for the hardening process. It is available in various types and colours. The two most common for modelling are the

Milliput and patterns made from it, standard and white milliput.

standard and the white. The standard is available from most hardware stores as it is sold for repairing various household objects, and the white from more specialist craft shops.

When the Milliput is completely hard it can be machined, drilled, tapped, sawn or turned. If working with it at normal temperature (20–25°C) within an hour it has a rubbery consistency; after 3–4 hours it is quite hard but a bit tacky; and if left overnight it becomes completely hard. The size and shape of the piece will vary the times, as if it is quite thick it will take longer for the middle to become firm. Heat can reduce the time it takes to set hard.

The standard Milliput is ideal for most jobs, but if you want to model fine intricate designs the white will be more suitable. It is important that the two compounds are mixed together thoroughly, as if they are not then sections will not set hard, making it difficult to carve and shape. This is easier to achieve with the standard as they are different colours, so you are able to see when the two parts are thoroughly mixed as they become one uniform colour instead of a marble effect. It is more difficult with the white as they are both very similar in colour. To ensure that both parts are thoroughly mixed with the white, knead together for at least five minutes.

When working with the Milliput try to form the main part of the shape while it is still soft, as it is more difficult when it has set hard. A lot of detail can also be incorporated while it is soft. You can use water with a brush or your finger to give the surface a smooth finish. Once it has dried it can be shaped with wax carving tools, files and a craft knife. To attain a very smooth finish use fine emery papers, 400 and then 600 grade, and then a fine wire wool. After using carving tools with the Milliput while it is soft, make sure you wash the tools thoroughly with warm soapy water before it has the opportunity to dry, as it will adhere to the surface of the tools and be difficult to remove.

The main difference between the standard Milliput and the white is that you can achieve much finer detail with the white. To put it simply the white is made up of a much finer grain that enables it to pick up much more detail and be worked more. The standard can be worked only a certain amount before cracking or falling apart; however even with this consideration it is possible to achieve some fine details with it. Another benefit working with the Milliput is that if it is shaped over formers and left to dry, once it is completely hard it will retain this shape, which can help to create some very intricate shapes.

Patterns made in pewter then developed further using car body filler.

Bird of Paradise clock, author.

WOOD

Wood can be carved, drilled, filed and emeryed, and it is recommended to seal with a varnish before using it to make a mould. It should be noted that if using a wood with a grain and then making a rubber mould, the rubber will pick up the details of the grain. If this is not an effect that will be needed the wood should be painted with a primer and sanded; several coats will probably be needed. MDF is a better alternative, although it will still need to be sealed, particularly if making a plaster mould. Note that a facemask should always be worn when cutting, filing or emerying MDF as the dust can be harmful if inhaled.

CAR BODY METAL FILLER

Metal filler can be useful for building up a shape. You start with a metal base and build up layers with the filler. As the filler has a large metal content it can then be filed and emeryed to achieve a smooth finish. You should only work with this material in a well-ventilated room.

There are lots of other materials that can be used as a pattern, such as Perspex, ceramic, foam board, resin or wire. It is just a matter of finding the one most suitable to the type of object that you want to make.

If your design is quite three-dimensional in shape you may want to consider whether the pattern needs to replicate the shape exactly, as a large mould can be expensive if you have to use a lot of rubber.

To make the Bird of Paradise Clock for example would need quite a large pattern which in turn would mean there would be a large mould. I wanted the curve to be quite deep to fit round the clock face, but this would entail making a very deep mould. So instead of making the pattern curved I made it flat. Then when it was cast in the pewter I shaped the casting around a former to fit with my design. As a result of this technique there was quite a thin rubber mould. For the second smaller leg of the clock I cut the tip off one of the castings, and filed and shaped it to the appropriate size. This also meant I did not have to make a second mould for the other supporting foot.

Bird of Paradise mould, pattern and casting.

Moulds

Given pewter's relatively low melting point in comparison to other metals, starting to melt at around 220°C up to 330°C, there is a wide variety of materials that can be used to make the moulds: cuttlefish, rubber, plaster, sand, metal, or wood.

Cuttlefish Mould

Cuttlefish casting is an ideal starting point to gain an understanding of casting with pewter. It is simple and results can be achieved quite quickly. It is the internal bone of a cuttlefish (*Sepia officinalis*) that is being used to make a two-part mould into which the molten metal can be poured. When dry cuttlefish has a chalky texture which can be easily cut and carved.

It is readily available from jewellery suppliers or from pet shops, where it is normally sold for pet birds to help keep the beak in good condition. If you are near the coast, particularly

the southern and western coast of Britain, quite often you can find cuttlefish bones washed up on the beach. To use these, rinse thoroughly in a weak bleach solution, which helps to reduce the smell, then leave in a warm place to dry thoroughly.

When casting silver into cuttlefish, the temperature has to be so high that it destroys the bone. However one of the advantages of casting pewter into cuttlefish is that the pewter temperature is relatively low, so if the shape is not too complicated and care is taken when removing the casting it is possible to get several castings from a single mould.

When designing something to be cast in a cuttlefish remember that the bone itself has a beautiful texture. It may look faint, but the pewter will pick up these details in the final casting, and this should be taken into account in the final design. If you are looking for a smooth finish an alternative mould material should be used.

EQUIPMENT
- Two cuttlefish bones of approximately the same size
- Jeweller's saw
- Coarse emery paper 120
- Pattern, made from a hard material
- Craft knife
- Wax carving tools
- Binding wire
- Pliers
- Torch or melting pot
- Ladle
- Metal tray

PREPARING THE CUTTLEFISH
You need to create two halves for the mould, so start with two cuttlefish bones. With the piercing saw cut off the top and bottom; the bone is soft and the saw will cut through it very easily. If you have got the bone from the pet shop or direct from the beach, you may find it has a brittle translucent edge, which should be removed. This can usually be done just with your hands, and any bone that will not come off can be removed with snips or scissors. If using a small pattern and the bone is quite large it is possible to use the one bone, cutting it in half across the middle.

One side of the bone will feel harder in comparison to the other. It is the soft side that is worked on to make the mould. Using a coarse emery paper place the soft side onto a flat surface and rub the bone across it until it is completely flat. Then repeat with the second bone. Once both bones have been sanded flat put them face to face to ensure you cannot see any light between them; if there are any gaps the pewter will not fill the mould without spilling out.

The simplest method for casting with cuttlefish is to use a pattern that is pushed into the bone to create a mould. The pattern will need to be made from a hard material; although the bone is relatively soft you will still need to exert some pressure to push the pattern into it, and you do not want it to become distorted or broken. Also ensure there are no undercuts as, unlike the rubber moulds, the bone has no flexibility to allow for them; the mould would be damaged as the pattern is pushed in.

USING A PATTERN WITH A FLAT BACK

Whether the pattern has a shape on both sides or has a flat back, the principles for setting up the mould and casting are the same.

Position the pattern so that it is not too close to the top of the bone. Then using an even pressure over the whole piece push the pattern into it. Push it into the bone until the flat back sits flush with the surface of the bone. Then using the brush, dust away the excess powder.

Gently remove the pattern. If it does not just fall from the mould when turned upside down, very gently tap the mould. Then using either the craft knife or the wax tool, position it at the top of the pattern in the middle, where the sprue will go, and gently lift the pattern out. (If you position the tool somewhere else around the mould it may cause damage which will show on the final casting, but the section where the sprue will be is going to be removed anyway.) You should now be left with the negative of your pattern in the bone.

It is time to create the pouring hole. Using a pencil draw a tapered pouring hole onto the bone, leading from the centre at the top of the cavity, with the widest section on the flat outside edge of the bone. Using a knife and wax tool cut out the section, creating half of a tapered funnel shape into the hollow. Once the cast is removed from the mould this funnel will have solidified into the sprue. A good guide to the depth and width of the sprue leading into the mould is that it should be as wide or as deep as the deepest part of your mould. If the pattern has a thin edge but is deeper in the middle, make a wide thin sprue; if the pattern is quite small or flat make a thin narrow one. If it is too small the pewter will cool and solidify in the sprue, so the casting will not be

Flat-backed pattern pressed into one half of the cuttlefish mould.

complete; but if it is too wide when it is removed from the final casting a lot of detail will be lost on that edge. This is particularly noticeable with the cuttlefish as it will obviously have the pattern of the bone on the casting which will be lost if cut off. Gently brush the dust from the pouring gate and blow any from the cavity.

Detail to show binding wire securing the mould together.

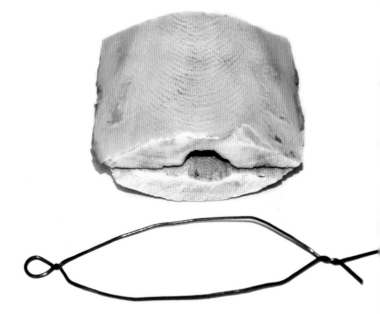

Place the two sanded cuttlefish together face to face and hold together with binding wire. Allow enough wire to go round both cuttlefish and be twisted to secure it in place. Fold the wire in half and create a small loop on the fold by twisting the wire a couple of times. Position the loop on the outside edge of the bone in the centre, then twist the wire on the opposite edge of the bone, using the pliers to twist the wires alternately. The loop enables both sides to be secured evenly and grips the two halves together more tightly and securely. Be careful not to over-twist the wire as it will snap. If it is a larger bone it may be necessary to wrap the wire around the top and bottom, as one may not be enough to stop the end flaring open when the pewter is poured in.

THE CASTING PROCESS

Place the bound cuttlefish in the middle of the metal tray, with firebricks around it so it will not fall over when the pewter is poured in. Position the tray close to the area where you will be casting, as it is important that the molten pewter is poured into the mould quickly without it cooling too much.

If using a melting pot set the temperature to approximately 290°C. Leave the ladle on the top edge of the pot, as this will help it to retain the heat. Alternatively if using a ladle, position the ladle on a fire-resistant sheet and build the bricks around it so it will not roll, because the pewter can start to move when it becomes molten.

Before beginning the casting process ensure you have followed the health and safety instructions and are wearing all the relevant protective equipment.

If using a melting pot, when the pewter has reached the right temperature, with an old tablespoon or scraper you need to remove the dross off the surface of the pewter. This is an oxide layer and if using pewter that has been used before it may also contain some of the talc and dirt from old castings, either of which will create imperfections in your castings if they are poured into the mould. Place an old tin at the side of the casting area to hold all the dross that is scraped off; this should not be re-used as it creates imperfections in castings made from it.

If using a torch and ladle start to heat the ladle, moving the flame around the outside and the inside. Melt the pewter until it is flowing freely as the ladle is moved and none is sticking to

Pouring the pewter into the cuttlefish mould.

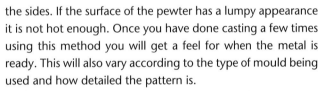

Open mould with the cast pattern.

Final casting with mould and original pattern.

the sides. If the surface of the pewter has a lumpy appearance it is not hot enough. Once you have done casting a few times using this method you will get a feel for when the metal is ready. This will also vary according to the type of mould being used and how detailed the pattern is.

Once the pewter is ready and the dross has been scraped off the surface, pour the pewter into the mould until a pool of pewter is created on the top of the cuttlefish; then the mould is full. Pour the pewter into the mould in a continuous movement. Do not stop halfway, then start again, as the pewter will start to cool at this point and this will create a weakness in the final casting where it could break off. If pouring from a melting pot, before pouring put the ladle into the pot and then pull it out. If the pewter sticks to the ladle it is not warm enough, so leave it in the pot for a few seconds until the ladle is so warm that the pewter runs straight off.

Leave the moulds to cool for a few minutes. You will see the change in the pewter pool on top of the mould: it will go from a shiny fluid surface to a matt finish. Once the pewter has cooled – this will take a few minutes – cut the binding wire and pull the two halves apart, using the pliers in case it is still hot. Gently remove the casting, taking care not to damage the mould, particularly if you want to re-use it.

When the casting has cooled cut off the sprue with a pair of flat-end cutters and clean the piece with a file and emery paper. To finish the piece it can either be polished on a bench polisher or put into a barrel polisher.

If making further castings gently brush the mould to remove any dust and repeat the process.

USING A ROUNDED PATTERN

With a pattern that has shape on both sides, the principles for setting up the mould and casting are the same as with the flat-back pattern. The main difference is when pressing the pattern into the mould you only push the pattern in halfway. It sometimes helps to make a mark on the pattern to indicate were the middle is. When the pattern is just under halfway in, cut some matches into four lengths of approximately 1cm pieces, depending upon the depth of the cuttlefish, and press them into the bone in the four corners around the pattern, again halfway. The matches act as locating pegs for the two halves, so they always align correctly. Using the second bone gently push it onto the pegs and the pattern, then squeeze them together so they lie flat against each other. Once the two halves lie flat, pull them apart and remove the pattern but not the matches. The mould is now ready for casting.

Cut the funnel as before on one half of the mould, then lightly dust the bone with graphite powder. Press the two halves together and cut out the second half of the funnel into the area that is clean of the graphite powder. (Talc cannot be used, as it will not show on the white bone.) Bind the two halves together as previously shown and place in the tray ready for casting.

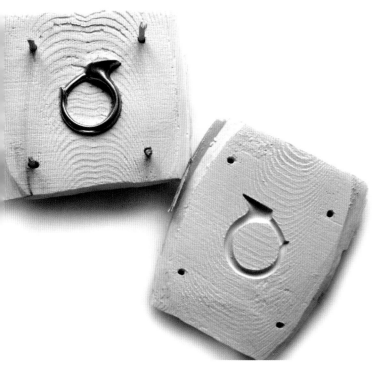

Ring pattern pushed into the bone and the locating pegs put in place.

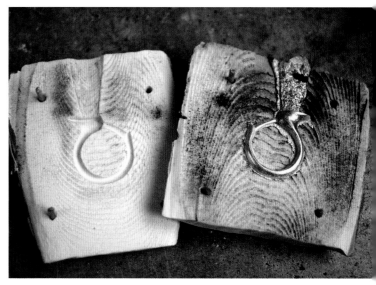

Cast ring.

EXERCISE

Making a Spoon

EQUIPMENT

■ 30mm disc 1.5mm thick pewter sheet
■ Dividers
■ Piercing saw
■ Files
■ Doming block and punches (either steel or wood)
■ Ball pein hammer
■ 400 emery paper
■ Two cuttlefish bones
■ Carving tools
■ Binding wire
■ Pliers
■ Length of 2mm wire with the end rounded
■ Ladle
■ Metal tray
■ Wire cutters
■ 180 grit sandpaper
■ Soft brush
■ One cabochon stone (preferably not larger than 2cm)

MAKING THE BOWL

Before casting the handle, the bowl for the spoon is made by hammering pewter sheet into a form. Set the dividers to 1.5cm and mark out a circle on a piece of pewter. Cut this out using the piercing saw. Then file around the edge. File off any sharp burs, using the doming block and punches. Select a dome and punch that is a suitable size for the disc; it is going to be quite a small shallow bowl, so do not select one that is too little, as the edge of the metal will fold and distort. Place the disc of pewter in the doming block. Using a ball pein hammer, strike the punch so the pewter is forced into the dome, moving the punch around the edges and down into the middle so the pewter eventually is in direct contact with the steel all the way round and you are left with a small shallow bowl suitable for a spoon.

Emery the top of the dome flat using a piece of emery paper on a flat surface. Then using the bench polisher, polish the dome on both sides doing the initial polish with the Hyfin (*see* Chapter 6). Very small mops are available for the bench polisher to get on the inside of the dome, or alternatively small mops can be used on a pendant or dremel drill.

Doming the bowl for the spoon.

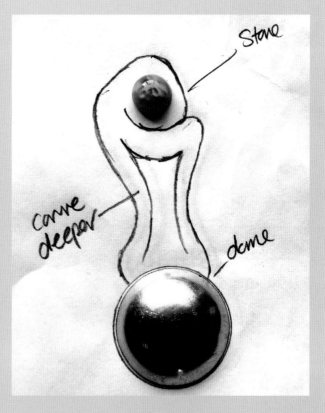

Design for the handle.

DESIGNING THE HANDLE AND CREATING THE PATTERN

(Note: For the purpose of this exercise the handle will have a flat back. Once you have gained more experience you can create a more three-dimensional shape.)

Place the dome on a piece of tracing or layout paper, then draw round the outside edge. Use this curve as the base for the spoon handle. This will ensure that the curve of the casting will fit neatly onto the pre-made dome for the bowl. Continue to design the handle shape, excluding the bowl part of the spoon. Be sure to consider how someone will hold it when it is being used. The cabochon stone will sit in the very top of the handle, so this should be allowed for in the design, making sure there is a minimum of 5mm space all around the stone in your final design.

Once the design has been finalized, place the pattern onto the cuttlefish, ensuring there is a minimum of 25cm from the top edge of the bone, with the end that the bowl will be soldered onto at the top of the bone. As

the bowl will be soldered onto here, none of the detail will be lost when the sprue is removed from the final casting.

Using a pencil that is not so sharp that it pierces through the paper, draw over the top of the pattern. When you remove the paper there should be an imprint of the design on the flat surface of the cuttlefish. You may want to go over the line again with the pencil to make it easier to see.

Use the carving tools to remove the bone to create the void for the pewter to flow into. Remember you are carving the reverse of what will come out in the pewter, so any lines carved into the bone will be raised on the final casting. For a solid handle that will not easily bend or distort carve to a minimum depth of 3mm. Carve the shape required, making sure there are no undercuts and leaving a flat area where the stone will be placed. Depending on the design it may be easier to cut the whole shape to a depth of 3mm and then start to work the detail into it.

Once complete put the stone into position. To make

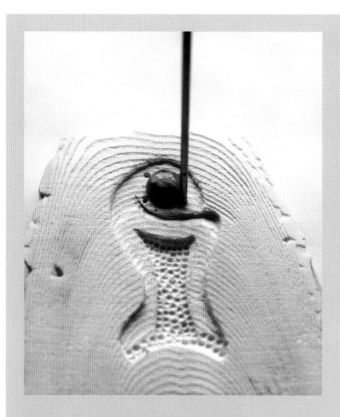

Detail showing the carved handle and making the claws to hold the stone in place.

CASTING THE HANDLE

The mould is now ready for casting. Ensure there is no dust or pieces of bone within the mould. Then, as shown previously, bind the carved half of the mould to the second bone and begin casting. It may be necessary to bind the top and bottom of the mould to stop it flaring open as the pewter is poured in.

When the final cast handle is done, cut off the sprue using the jeweller's saw. Then using a half round or oval file, clean the area where the sprue was. Remove the end so the domed bowl that was previously made sits neatly on the handle.

When happy that there is a clean joint, use firebricks to position the two pieces and solder the bowl onto the handle. (*See* Chapter 2.)

After the soldering is completed rinse off the flux with hot soapy water, then put the whole piece into the barrel polisher (*see* Chapter 6) for a final polish. Leave it in the polisher for 30–45 minutes.

Pushing the claws over the stone on the final polished casting.

the claws that will hold the stone, with a pencil mark four spots equally spaced around the stone. Then using the 2mm wire with the round end push it into the bone in each of the four positions. The depth will obviously depend on the height of the stone; if it is small and shallow you may want to make it less deep. The pegs will be pushed over the stone so make them long enough to do this, but they should not be too long; there should be just enough to hold the stone in place. It is better to make the pegs slighter longer as they can always be cut to size, but not as easy to rectify if they are too short. Make sure the wire is pushed in at a 90-degree angle, as if it is not, it will create an undercut and the mould will be damaged when the casting is removed.

For surface decoration on the handle you can do this with the carving tools, or use an old biro to create a beaded edge. You may want to experiment using various tools or instruments to create different patterns. When the carving is completed mark out the sprue as explained when making the rounded pattern mould and cut this out, again in the funnel shape.

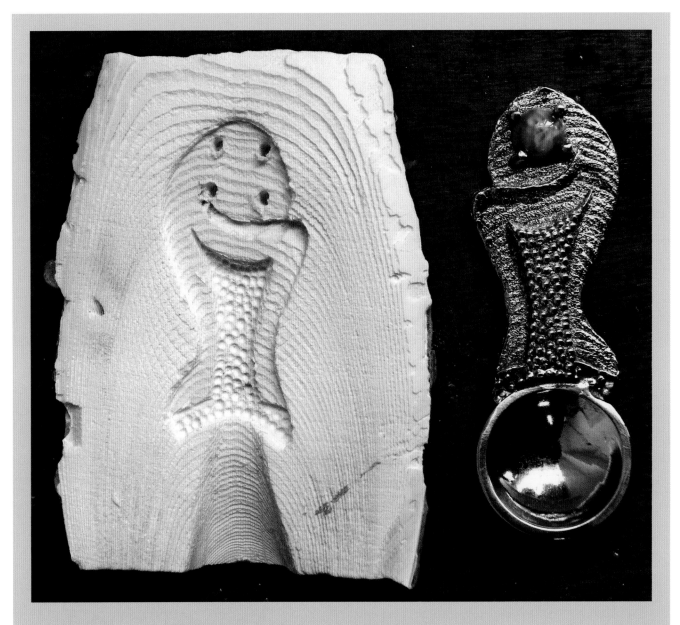

The cuttlefish mould and finished spoon.

As there is so much detail due to the spoon being cast in the cuttlefish you may want to highlight this by using the blackening technique. If colouring the spoon this should be done now, prior to the stone being set (*see* Chapter 4).

The spoon is now ready for the stone to be set into it. Place the stone between the four pegs. It is at this point the length of the pegs should be checked; they do not want to be too long once pushed over the stone, there should be just enough to hold the stone in place.

Using a wooden stick, as this will not mark the pewter like metal would, start to push the claws over the stone. It is quite easy to push them over in one go, but try to do it in stages to make sure the stone is positioned centrally between them. If one claw is pushed all the way over the stone in one movement the stone will move off centre.

The spoon is now finished and ready to be used.

Rubber Mould

Silicone rubbers are available that will cure at room temperature and withstand higher temperatures, room temperature vulcanizing rubber (RTV rubber). There are many advantages to using this rubber. If the mould is used correctly it is possible to get several thousand castings from it. It has flexibility so the pattern can have slight undercuts, but if they are deep these areas of rubber will be weak and the rubber will eventually tear. As it is not heat-treated and there is very little shrinkage you are not limited to the type of material used for making the pattern, so even using an organic material is possible. Most importantly the finish is very good, and very intricate detailed pieces can be made.

The rubber comes as a liquid and needs a catalyst to trigger the curing process. It is designed to be able to withstand temperatures of up to 260°C for long periods of time and up to 316°C for shorter periods, which is ideal for casting pewter.

Mixing the Rubber

Mix the rubber in the tin. Then pour some of the rubber into the mixing jug, trying to avoid excessive air being put into it; you may want to wear rubber gloves as it can be quite messy. Gently stir the rubber, then add the catalyst; it is recommended to add 3–5 per cent of catalyst to the rubber, and this works out at approximately nine to fifteen drops per 100g of rubber.

Once the catalyst has been added thoroughly mix it into the rubber. This is very important, as if it is not mixed well enough, parts of the mould will not cure properly leaving it in a liquid state and unsuitable for casting into. If 3 per cent of catalyst is added the rubber will start thickening within 80 minutes and cured in 24 hours; when adding 5 per cent catalyst the pot life is approximately 48 minutes and cured in about 5 hours depending on the size of the mould. The room temperature can affect the process: a cold temperature will increase the curing time whereas a warm environment will reduce it.

It is possible to speed up the curing process by simply adding water, approximately one drop of water to three drops of catalyst; again it should be mixed thoroughly to avoid pockets of water being trapped in the rubber.

EXERCISE

Making an Egg Holder

This exercise is to make an egg holder. It is described as a holder for the simple reason that it holds the egg in place rather than 'cupping' the egg as usual. To cast the feet it uses a two-part mould, which is suitable for more three-dimensional shapes. The part that holds the egg is made by hand-forming pewter sheet. It will also incorporate some of the previous working techniques such as piercing, sawing and soldering.

Before starting you will need to select an object that can be used as a pattern to make the feet of the holder; this can be something you have already designed or it can be a found object. This exercise uses a toy tortoise. When selecting an object for the feet consider whether it will raise the height of the holder enough so that when the egg is in it, it will not be resting on the table. It is possible to select a smaller item, for example a shell, and instead of casting one for each side of the holder, you can cast several and solder them together to increase the height.

MAKING A TWO-PART MOULD

EQUIPMENT

- Flat surface such as a glass or a ceramic tile
- RTV101 Rubber and catalyst
- Lego bricks, card or foam board (Lego is more practical)
- Plasticine/Chavant
- Silicon Release Spray
- Pattern

When a pattern has been selected or made, draw a line around the middle, then position on the tile. Start to build a wall in Lego around the pattern, allowing a minimum of 1.5cm space all around the edge of the pattern and a minimum of 2.5cm at the top of the pattern where the pewter will be poured in, to allow space for the sprue, which will allow the pewter to be poured into the mould. Careful consideration should be given to where the best place will be to position the sprue on the pattern, as the sprue will obviously need to be cut off on the final casting and you will not want any important details to be lost while

Egg holders showing variations for the feet.

doing this. The wall should be built to a minimum of 1cm above the highest point of the pattern. It is important to remember that molten metal will be poured into the mould and if it is too thin when the mould is clamped together it will distort the mould, making inaccurate castings.

Fill the bottom of the box with Plasticine or Chavant, leaving space for your pattern in the middle. (Chavant is a sulphur-free, oil-based sculpting clay which is non-drying;

Ensure the pattern is set into the Chavant/Plasticine correctly.

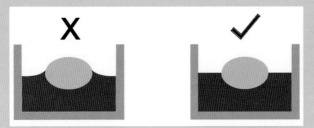

it usually requires some heat, 44–55°C, to soften it to make it easy to work with, and using water can help to smooth the surface.) Position the pattern in the Plasticine and build the Plasticine to halfway up, then make the surface as flat as possible leading from the pattern to the Lego wall.

Make sure that the Plasticine butts up to the edge of the pattern and the Lego wall, leaving no gaps for the rubber to leak underneath. It is important to ensure the Plasticine meets the pattern at a right angle. The Plasticine will eventually be the second half of your rubber mould; if it tapers to a thin edge this will also be very thin in the rubber and likely to tear when using it for casting the pewter.

Make the surface of the Plasticine as smooth as possible. Then using a doming punch or something with a rounded head, push it into each corner. These will be the keys so that the two halves align correctly. If Plasticine has been used you can help to stop any rubber sticking to it by lightly spraying the surface with the silicon release spray and leaving it for a couple of minutes to dry.

Finding the high point on a pattern.

Once the rubber has been brushed onto the pattern the rubber can be poured in from the corner.

ACCOMMODATING THE HIGH POINTS

If you are using an irregular shape for a pattern and you want to ensure the two halves pull away easily you will need to plot the high points on your pattern. Lay the pattern on a flat surface, using a piece of Plasticine to hold it in place if it moves around. Take a set square and move it around the shape, marking off all the high points with a pen where the pattern touches the set square. Once you have gone around the whole pattern join all the marks together like a dot-to-dot so a line is drawn around the whole pattern. Using this line you can then set the pattern in the Plasticine taking the Plasticine up to this line. It may look very irregular, but all the high points will have been accounted for and when the pewter is poured, the mould will not be forced to stretch over any undercuts, so increasing the life of your mould.

Mix the rubber as described previously, enough to fill up the box to about 1cm above the highest point of the pattern. Once the rubber has been mixed with the catalyst, brush a thin layer onto the surface of the pattern to ensure that the rubber is completely covering the surface and any intricate details. If it is poured straight in, little air holes can be created, and when the rubber dries and the pewter is poured in, these little holes will fill with pewter and leave tiny little pewter balls on the surface of the casting.

Gently tap the box to force any air bubbles to the surface. Then starting in one corner continue to fill the box, ensuring it is a minimum of 1cm above the height of the pattern. When the box is full, gently agitate the box to force any trapped air to the surface. Then leave the rubber to cure. If it can be left overnight it is better, to ensure it has set completely.

When the rubber is ready, remove the Lego wall. Turn over the box and gently peel back the Plasticine without removing the pattern. Some of the rubber may have leaked a little bit into the gaps of the Lego wall; these can easily be removed with a craft knife.

Once the rubber is completely clean, lightly spray the surface and the sides with silicone release spray; this is in case there are any leaks down the sides. Then leave to dry for a couple of minutes. It is very important to remember to do this, as if not, the rubber will adhere itself to the first half and will be impossible to pull apart.

Rebuild the Lego wall again, allowing a space of about 1cm above the highest point of the pattern. The mould is now ready to pour in the second half as done previously.

Once the mould is set, the Lego wall can be removed and the two halves can be pulled apart. Start in one corner and slowly peel the two halves apart around the edge, before completely pulling them apart; this will minimize the risk of tearing the mould.

Using talc to create a mark for cutting out the pouring gate.

You now need to cut a pouring gate into the rubber, but it will also need to be duplicated on the second half of the mould, so a complete cone shape is created instead of a half. Start with a small-size hole where it enters the cavity and increase it later if that is what is needed.

As the molten pewter cools, the mould draws in the pewter from the sprue. This creates a pitted, porous surface to the sprue. If this were to happen within the actual mould it would ruin the surface of the casting, so the funnel shape needs to be larger on the outside of the mould but relatively small going into the cavity. The larger sprue enables this process to happen outside of the actual casting area.

To ensure that both holes are in the same place, once the first half has been cut out, lightly dust it with talc or graphite powder, dust off the excess, then put the two halves together and gently squeeze. When the two halves are pulled apart the graphite will have stuck to the surface everywhere except for where the rubber has been cut away. Use these lines as a guide for cutting the second half.

When cutting the rubber to stop the rubber tearing use a sharp knife and try to use as much of the depth of the rubber as possible, so when the two halves are together the hole at the top is quite large to pour the pewter in but when looking into the mould the hole actually going into the cavity is relatively small.

The mould is then ready to be used for casting. Clamp the two halves between the MDF. Position the mould about 1cm below the edge of the wood; by doing this any excess pewter will flow down the sides of the mould instead of over the top of the wood and the clamps.

Gravity Casting into a Rubber or Plaster Mould

EQUIPMENT
■ Mould, either plaster or rubber
■ Metal tray
■ Melting pot/torch and ladle
■ Talc, French chalk or graphite powder
■ Face shield and long arm leather gloves

Open mould showing the casting.

Two-part rubber mould: pouring the pewter.

Position the mould in the middle of the tray, ensuring it is supported and will not fall over while the pewter is being poured.

When pouring the pewter it is vital that it is poured in one attempt into the mould. If the mould is only half full you cannot then pour into it again, as the pewter will have already started to cool and when it is removed from the mould it will simply break apart. So ensure the ladle is large enough to hold enough pewter to pour in one go. If using a melting pot leave the ladle in the pot for a few minutes to heat up, because if the ladle is not warm the pewter will start to cool as soon as it is put into it, thus reducing the temperature of the molten metal before it has a chance to reach the mould. The pewter should flow cleanly off the ladle. If it sticks, the ladle is too cool.

At this point put on your face shield and gloves. If using a torch, before pouring, take an old spoon or scraper and clean the pewter surface of any dross, then quickly pour it into the mould. If taking the pewter from the melting pot, clean the surface, then dip the ladle deep into the pot to ensure you are getting clean pewter, and quickly but carefully pour the pewter into the mould.

When the mould is full the pewter will pool on the surface of the sprue hole that has been cut into the mould. As the pewter cools you can see the metal cooling; when molten it will have a mirror-like finish and as it cools it will become matt. Leave it for a few minutes to cool before opening the mould.

When you have two good castings, or more if you are soldering several together, cut off the sprues, clean them with a file and emery paper, removing any thin flashing around the edge with a sharp knife. If it is a new mould it may be necessary to do several castings, and also if the mould is cold doing a few castings will warm it up. The casting can then be put into a barrel polisher for 30–45 minutes.

PROBLEMS

The mould is not filling with pewter? This could be caused by various reasons. (1) The pewter is not warm enough: it is not being poured quickly enough into the mould and is cooling before it reaches it. (2) The mould has a small amount of pewter in the bottom of the mould and a plug in the sprue: the pouring gate may not be large enough; using the craft knife carefully increase the size of the pouring gate, doing it a little bit at a time.

Certain parts of the mould consistently do not fill with pewter? This could be caused by air becoming trapped. It may be necessary to make a small vent, beginning at the problem area then moving up away from the negative space. A sprue cutter is ideal for this, but if one is not available a craft knife can be used. The vent only needs to be very thin – just large enough to allow the air to escape. If using a knife make sure it is sharp so it does not drag and tear the rubber.

Intricate surface detail is coming out quite rounded and not very sharp on the final casting? This is likely to be caused by the pewter not being warm enough. Try increasing the temperature.

The rubber has torn? It is possible to glue the torn rubber with glue specifically made for rubber. This area does however become a weak point, and extra care will be needed when pulling the mould apart or removing the casting.

Making the Holder

EQUIPMENT

- Pewter sheet 1.5 to 2mm thick, 9.5cm x 11cm
- Piercing saw
- Flat file and a half round or oval file
- Emery stick
- Rawhide mallet
- Round wooden former with a shallow curve, approximately 14cm diameter
- Bench polisher

Make a template for a large oval that will use the whole piece of pewter. Use this to transfer the shape onto the pewter. Cut out the oval using the jeweller's saw, and neaten up the edges with the flat file and then emery stick. Make sure all the burrs (sharp bits of metal) are removed, as when shaping it on the wooden former burrs may damage the surface of the wood.

A wooden bowling ball is used as the former, as this is an ideal shape. The pewter needs to be curved the full length of the piece, but also across the oval as well. This creates a better profile and it also increases the strength of the bridge it will become.

Using a rawhide mallet hammer the ends of the holder over the former.

After marking the circle using a template pierce out the hole ready to hold the egg.

Position the oval centrally on top of the former. Place both hands at either end of the former, then using an even pressure gently bend the pewter until it is curved around the former.

Using the mallet hammer the end of the oval onto the former so it sits closer to the ball, then turn the oval round and do the opposite end. Where the two ends have been hammered there will be a kink in the line, both ends and both sides of the oval. Resting the oval about 3mm above the ball start to hammer the long top outside edge down onto the ball; keep checking the profile as you are hammering to see that there is a nice smooth curve without any raised lumps. The aim is to create a gentle downward curve on the edges, which you should be able to see if looking at the holder from either of the two ends.

Be careful to only hammer the very outside edge of the upper surface of the oval; the curve is literally along the edges, and you must avoid mallet marks all over the top of the pewter as these would all need to be removed. Try to mark the pewter as little as possible. Do both outside lengths of the oval until it rests neatly on the former without any visible gaps.

Once the hammering is complete run around the outside edge of the oval with the emery paper, as the mallet may have stretched some areas, creating small raised areas. If the mallet has marked the outside edge of the surface this will also need to be emeried flat again, as when it is polished the mop will follow the surface, creating a rippled edge.

When the emerying is complete the back and front of the curved oval can be polished on a bench polisher, being careful when polishing the back not to catch the curved ends on the mop. The polishing can be saved until the circle has been cut out for the egg to sit in, but this makes it more difficult to polish as the gap between the hole and the outside edge is quite small and also as the mop may catch on the hole and the whole shape can be distorted very easily.

When the polishing is complete a hole needs to be made to hold the egg. Using the oval template made earlier, mark off the centre, then mark a circle with a diameter of 4cm. Place the template over the oval and using a scriber draw round the inside of the template. Do not cut out the hole prior to bending the oval, as it will become a distorted oval in shape and will then not hold an egg.

Using a pillar drill with a small drill bit (large enough for a jeweller's saw blade) drill a hole on the inside of the line. It will be awkward while drilling because of the curve, so make sure that the oval is supported so that the pressure of the drill does not distort its shape.

The hole will now need to be cut out. Unscrew one end of the saw and place the blade through the hole with the scribed circle facing away from you. Compress the frame, then tighten the nut, making sure there is tension in the blade. If the blade is not taut enough it will snag very easily and break. Start to cut around the inside edge of the line. This will be quite difficult because of the curved form. Once the whole circle has been cut out, use an oval or half round file and then an emery stick to neaten the edge, remembering to remove the burr.

It is advisable at this stage to check that an egg sits in the hole comfortably before trying to solder it onto the feet. If the egg is wobbling or sitting at an angle you should be able to see where the problem is as the area will be raised. Mark it with a pencil so you know where to file when the egg is removed.

Before soldering the oval to the feet, work out the position for the oval onto the feet. Then with a piece of emery, clean the area on the oval and the foot, where the solder joint will be. This removes any dirt and leaves a clean area for the solder to flow.

If you have cast several small items that will be put together to make a foot, solder them together before soldering the foot onto the oval.

When soldering take care as the casting is thicker and heavier than the oval it is being soldered onto, so it will need more heat to create a balance between the two pieces so that the solder flows evenly between the two. If you have any castings that were not successful it is a good idea to practise by soldering a piece of sheet onto a piece of casting prior to attempting the actual piece. This helps to get a feel for how much heat is needed and where to position the torch – as otherwise you could melt it by mistake.

Brush the flux over the two surfaces. Then either cut small paillons of solder and position along the seam or, if stick soldering, have it ready. Start to heat the piece directing the flame predominantly onto the casting; the heat should be enough to transfer onto the oval without having to point the torch on it directly. When all the solder has flowed leave the holder to cool completely; the casting can retain a lot of heat, enough to keep the solder at a pasty stage for several minutes, so if moved, the oval will separate from the casting.

Once the holder is cool, wash it in hot soapy water to remove the flux and then give it a final polish with a soft mop and rouge.

Pewter is a traditional material with limitless possibilities. Here function meets form with a quirky bowl. **Carrol Boyes** started designing and making pewter cutlery from her basement in South Africa 18 years ago. Today this small-scale business has become a large company employing 350 people and her work is sold worldwide.

Rajesh Gogna is a silversmith who produces one-off pieces and commissions normally working in silver. His Writing Instrument was an exploration of pewter and the casting process. Inspired by the quill it is an ergonomic, functional piece which is comfortable to use with the left or right hand.

Writing Instrument, Rajesh Gogna.

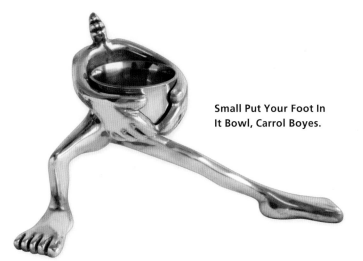

Small Put Your Foot In It Bowl, Carrol Boyes.

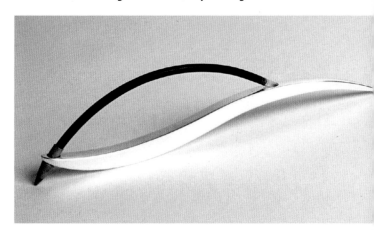

One-part mould with cast coaster.

Making a One-Part Rubber Mould

A one-part mould is ideal when making items such as a coaster, medal or a picture frame where the back is completely flat and has no detail. It can have some undercuts if made with a rubber mould.

EQUIPMENT
- Pattern
- Ceramic or glass tile
- Lego bricks, card or foam board (Lego is more practical)
- Mixing jug and knife
- RTV101 Rubber
- Brush
- Talc/graphite powder
- Two pieces of MDF slightly larger than the object you will be casting
- One G-clamp
- Tray
- Rubber gloves

Place the pattern on the tile. If the object is quite light and may move as the rubber is poured in, it is advisable to secure it with some double-sided tape so it does not float into the rubber, making it unsuitable for casting. Build a wall in Lego around the pattern, as for the two-part mould (see page 46).

When the pattern is ready mix enough rubber to fill the Lego box, as described above. To avoid air bubbles being formed on the surface of the mould when the rubber has been mixed, paint a thin layer onto the surface of the pattern using a brush. (The brush can be cleaned later with white spirit.)

When the pattern is completely covered gently tap the tile on the worktop. This will bring any air bubbles to the surface. Starting from a corner slowly pour the remainder of the rubber into the box. Once the box is full gently tap the box on the surface for a few minutes to encourage any air bubbles to rise to the surface. If there is not enough rubber mixed to fill the box it is possible to add extra; just repeat the process and pour on top.

Once the mould has completely cured (solidified) a pouring gate has to be cut into the rubber. Find a suitable spot where not too much detail will be lost and cut a half funnel shape into the rubber leading from the pattern to the edge of the mould. It is better to make the hole smaller and try casting into it as it can always be made bigger if it is found to be too small and the pewter solidifies in the sprue before filling the mould. It is however more difficult to add rubber to it again if the sprue has been made too large. Try casting it a few times to see if it is suitable before increasing the size.

When the sprue has been cut into the rubber lightly dust the mould with either talc or graphite powder. Then clamp the rubber mould between the two pieces of MDF. Place the rubber about 1cm below the edge of the two pieces of wood. This stops any excess pewter flowing over the top onto the clamps, leaving it free to run down the sides into the tray instead.

The MDF facing the rubber will make the smooth surface of the back of the casting, and the MDF on the outer side of the rubber will make an even hard surface to clamp the whole mould together. Do not screw the clamps too tightly as this will distort the negative space within the mould and create irregular castings; the clamps should very gently hold everything in place.

The mould is now ready to pour the pewter into it (*see* page 49).

Gedeo Siligum

Silicone rubber can be used for either a one-part or two-part mould, as it is a putty rather than liquid and has a much faster curing time. Gedeo Siligum is a silicone rubber and hardens in ten minutes. It is ideal for making a mould which needs to be done quickly. As it is a putty it is more difficult to prevent small air holes in the mould, but they can be avoided if care is taken during the mould-making process. It is also more expensive in comparison to the RTV rubber; it is available in 100g and 300g pots, and the price of a 300g pot of Siligum is the equivalent in price to a 1kg pot of the RTV.

This said, it is great for making moulds quickly, and if the mould is made carefully without any deep undercuts it is possible to get a several hundred castings from the one mould. It is also very simple to use. It comes in two parts: one blue and one white. The two parts should be mixed equally for about thirty seconds until they have become a uniform colour with no streaks of colour; this is to ensure the whole mould hardens. When the rubber is mixed it has a working time of about five minutes and will be set completely hard in ten. This time can shorten if working in a warm environment. So with Siligum it is possible to make a two-part mould ready for casting in about half an hour.

As Siligum goes hard at room temperature, this enables a variety of materials to be used as a pattern. If a Siligum mould is made well it is possible to use very detailed pieces as a pattern, as the rubber will pick it all up. Siligum is completely harmless: there are no fumes, it is not harmful if in contact with skin and it is a clean material to work with.

There is another silicone rubber called Quick-Sil, which will set hard in fifteen minutes. This is relatively cheap, being the same price for 2kg as 300g of the Siligum. It can however be very difficult to work with, leaving quite large air pockets in the rubber when it has set. You can try various methods, such as using weights on top of the rubber as it sets to force the air out, but as yet I have not had success in attaining an air bubble-free mould.

Making a Two-Part Mould with Siligum

EQUIPMENT
- Tile
- Lego
- Gedeo Siligum
- Wooden clay tool
- Silicon release spray
- Craft knife
- Doming punch

When using the rubber to make a mould, prepare a tile in the same way as for an RTV mould. Build a Lego wall around the pattern with a minimum of 1cm gap between the wall and the pattern; this helps to contain the rubber and create a neat mould.

Mix the rubber and make it into a smooth ball. Push the pattern into the ball, not too deep, still coming halfway up the pattern and leaving about 1cm of rubber behind the pattern. Try to push the pattern slowly into the rubber using a gentle pressure from the centre to the outside edge; this ensures the pattern is pushed into the rubber so it will pick up the detail and it also assists in trying to force any air out of the mould.

The ball shape is ideal as it creates a smooth surface to push the pattern into. Do not try to put the rubber on the pattern a bit at a time; if the rubber starts to harden before you have had a chance to cover the whole pattern there will be small creases where the rubber has been patched together, and these will show on any casting made from the mould.

Place the rubber and the pattern into the box and spread the excess rubber filling the box using your finger and a wooden clay tool. If the rubber moves up the sides of the pattern use the tool to push it back down, remembering to make the rubber come away from the pattern at a 90-degree angle not sloping away (*see* page 46). Before the rubber has hardened, push the doming punch part way into the rubber

Lego set-up with Siligum and pattern, pushing in the doming punch to make the locating keys.

at the four corners; these dimples will make the keys to hold the mould together in the correct position. If you find there is not enough rubber to fill the box it is possible to mix some more and add it but, as noted previously, avoid doing this in the area directly surrounding the pattern as it will create small seams in the rubber that will then show in the final pewter castings.

Leave the rubber to harden for about ten minutes. Then

spray the surface of the rubber and pattern with the silicone release spray; leave it for a couple of minutes to allow the spray to dry.

Then repeat the process: mix the rubber, make into a ball, then again starting from the centre use a gentle pressure pushing the rubber down towards the outside edge of the pattern and to the sides of the box, trying to make the surface of the rubber as flat as possible. Leave it again for ten minutes to harden.

Once the rubber has become hard the Lego wall can be removed. Then using the wooden clay tool find where the two halves meet and slowly work around the whole outside edge of the mould to release them from each other. Then inserting your thumbs between the two slowly start to pull them apart, being careful not to do it too quickly and tear the mould.

Once you have both halves of the mould you will need to cut the pouring gate (*see* page 48), making a cone shape larger on the outside of the mould and very small where the sprue becomes the casting. Once the first half has been cut it can be transferred onto the second half using the graphite powder or talc and then cut again. You should then have a two-part mould with a pouring gate. Brush the surface of the mould with talc and it is then ready to have the pewter poured into it.

Finished moulding paste mould and Milliput pattern.

Seaweed on a Beach sculpture, carved walnut and pewter,
author (photographer Steve Speller).

some fine adjustments. By making a plaster mould, then casting the piece in the pewter, you can adjust it accordingly until you have a complete pattern ready to make a rubber mould from. This means you are not making costly preparation rubber moulds.

There are many types of plaster available. The most basic is suitable for making a mould that does not have lots of detail and only needs to be used a few times. However if casting more intricate details a harder plaster may be more suitable. Most ceramic suppliers will stock the various types.

WORKING WITH PLASTER

Wear a dust mask and latex gloves when mixing plaster.

After working with plaster wash off any plaster dust. Some people can be particularly sensitive to the plaster, so direct contact should be avoided.

Working with plaster can be messy, so any exposed surfaces may need to be covered.

Polythene bowls are preferable for mixing in as they have a flexibility that will make it easier to remove any dry plaster. Wear old clothes, as set plaster can be difficult to remove.

Never pour plaster down a sink, as it can set and block the waste pipes.; once it has set, any excess plaster can be poured into a plastic bag for disposal.

Creating a Plaster Mould

Casting into a plaster mould is an inexpensive way of making a mould if making a one-off piece or you just require a few castings. When designing a piece or choosing a pattern it is important to remember that the plaster has no flexibility so there should be no undercuts.

Plaster casting is ideal for creating larger one-off pieces like this sculptural piece, Seaweed on a Beach. As this piece was quite large, approximately 50cm long and about 5cm thick at the widest point, it would have been very expensive to make it in rubber, particularly as only one casting was needed.

The size did cause other problems such as getting all the pewter into the mould in one fluid movement. Without a ladle large enough it took two people filling ladles and pouring the pewter together. The casting came out better once the mould had been used several times, after it had become warm.

A plaster mould can also be useful if you have a wax or Milliput pattern for a design, where you would like to make

Making a Two-Part Plaster Mould

EQUIPMENT
- Original pattern
- Lego or larger plastic children's bricks
- Plasticine, clay or Chavant
- Plaster
- Water
- Bucket or bowl for mixing
- Dust mask
- Plastic gloves
- Model maker's size or petroleum jelly

Once a pattern has been selected, building the box to contain the plaster and setting up the pattern is the same as making a two-part rubber mould (*see* page 46). It is very important with the plaster mould to ensure that you allow for any high points on the pattern as any undercuts will cause the plaster to break when it is being removed.

Plaster is an ideal material for making a large mould. If making a bigger mould it is possible to use larger children's bricks, ensuring the corner bricks are all interlinked so they cannot be forced apart when the plaster is being poured in. If making an even larger mould, using wooden mould boards as used in ceramic work will be more appropriate. As it is larger in scale you can use clay to embed the pattern in the bottom of the box up to the centre line drawn around the shape. Roll thin sausage shapes of clay and push them into the corners on the outside of the box. This will also ensure that none of the plaster will leak out of the box as it is being poured.

Before building the wall establish where the sprue will be. Unlike the rubber mould it is necessary to leave more space between the pattern and the wall; a minimum of 4cm around the edge is a good guideline, with possibly more at the top where the sprue will be. The depth of the plaster above the highest point of the pattern should also be increased to a minimum of 3cm. These are just guidelines and may need to be varied depending on the size and shape of the pattern.

Each type of plaster comes with its own specific ratio for the quantities used when mixing with water, and better results will be achieved by following the guidelines given. The general basic ratio is usually three parts water to two parts plaster. A simple way is to sprinkle handfuls of plaster into the bucket of water until the plaster creates a peak above the waterline. The plaster is always added to the water, while wearing a dust mask.

Once the plaster has been added to the water it will set hard within 20 minutes; if warm water is used this will speed up the process.

When the plaster has been added, leave for one minute and allow the plaster to absorb the water. Then either using your hand (wearing gloves) or a stick thoroughly mix the plaster; doing it by hand is better as you are able to feel the consistency of the plaster and feel if there are any lumps within the mix. Stir the plaster in a wide circular movement, occasionally turning the palm and lifting the plaster; this can help to release any air.

The plaster is ready to pour when a line can be drawn across the surface and it starts to hold. When this occurs, starting from one corner pour the plaster into the box. As the plaster starts to set there will be a noticeable increase in temperature within the plaster and it will be warm to touch.

Once the plaster is completely hard and the box built around it can be removed, peel off the clay (Plasticine or Chavant). Then if Lego or the larger bricks have been used, using an old straight steel ruler or knife draw it down the edge of the plaster mould to neaten up the sides.

Box set-up with pattern: plaster ready to be mixed and poured over the pattern.

Locating keys will then be needed to key the two halves of the mould together. This can be done simply by holding a spoon vertically then twisting it into the plaster, and this will create a dimple shape within the plaster.

The mould will then need to be treated to stop the plaster sticking to itself when pouring the second half. Soft soap is traditionally used in ceramics; the soft soap is thinned down with water, then brushed onto the surface of the plaster and around the sides with a sponge. Leave to dry for a few minutes then apply a second coat; it is likely that 2–3 coats will be needed. The plaster should have a smooth, shiny finish so that when put under a tap water flows straight over the surface rather than being absorbed. Petroleum jelly and oil can also be used as a barrier if soft soap is not available.

The wall is then built again and the process of mixing the plaster and pouring it into the box is repeated. When the mould is completely hard remove the wall and carefully separate the two halves. The plaster expands slightly when it goes through the warm stage; this is an ideal time to remove the pattern.

It is possible to cut the sprue into the plaster while it is wet using a knife or a rasp (a wire brush may be needed to clean the rasp as it will become clogged with the plaster quite quickly, or alternatively wait until the plaster is completely dry). A funnel shape should be made, starting small at the edge of the pattern and expanding towards the edge of the plaster similar to that in the rubber mould.

For your safety…

MOISTURE IN THE PLASTER MOULD

Before the plaster mould can be used for casting it is very important that the plaster must be completely dry. Any moisture within the mould will react with the molten pewter and will trigger an explosive reaction causing hot pewter to explode out of the mould and into the surrounding area.

The mould should be left in a warm room to dry; next to a radiator or in an airing cupboard would be suitable. This can take several days. It is possible to put it in an oven on minimum heat for several hours with the door slightly open to release the moisture that comes from the mould. If using this method the oven should not be turned up too high as it will cause the plaster to dry too quickly, which will give the

plaster a powdery brittle texture that will ruin the surface of the mould.

Once the mould is completely dry it is ready. Brush the mould with talc or graphite powder. Gently clamp it together; putting wood either side of the mould will help to spread the pressure of the clamp so minimizing the risk of it cracking. Position it within the metal tray and it is then ready for the pewter to be poured in.

Casting into a Carved Plaster Mould

This is a simple project, to make small flat-back castings, in this case making cast sections for pieces of jewellery. It uses a plaster block, made by building a wall of building bricks, then pouring the plaster directly into a sectioned-off area. The

Carving the pattern into the dried plaster using wax carving tools.

The plaster block sandwiched between two pieces of wood clamped together and the pewter poured in.

plaster is then left to dry. When the block is thoroughly dry it should be emeryed on a flat plate with a coarse sandpaper on both sides to ensure it is completely flat.

Shapes can be cut into the plaster with wax carving tools, similar to the method used for casting into the cuttlefish bone. The advantage to this method is that there will be a smooth surface unlike the cuttlefish casting where the molten pewter picks up the detail of the bone.

If it is a large block and the shape is carved in the middle the pewter may have a long way to travel and will cool too quickly, so carve the pattern near to the edge. When the shape/shapes are complete, make a pouring hole from the outside of the plaster to the negative space again using the funnel shape, large to small from the outside of the plaster. The plaster is then sandwiched between two pieces of wood and held together with a clamp ready for the pewter to be poured in.

The finished castings, mould and a necklace produced with the castings, which castings have been blackened then polished and combined with haematite beads.

59

The steel former ready to be dipped into the molten pewter.

Pewter has now coated the former.

Dip Casting

This technique uses a steel form that is plunged into the molten pewter and a skin of pewter forms over the tool. The longer the tool is left in the thicker the layer becomes. However care must be taken because if the steel becomes too warm the pewter drops off.

One designer to employ the dip-casting technique is **Tim Parsons**. Normally when used in a commercial environment the item has been dipped and the rough surface is removed on a lathe. He investigated ways to make unique objects using these manufacturing processes. He dipped vases in pewter and then fitting the vases into a lathe he removed part of the rough surface to create a coastline transition between the rough and the smooth that was different on each piece.

PROBLEMS

This process is very unpredictable. At a low temperature approximately 240°C the pewter is quite cool so will create a thick spiky wall. Between 270°C and 280°C are preferable working temperatures.

Size and shape of former? It is advisable to do some experimenting with each former, as there are various factors that can alter the end result, such as size and thickness. If the

Finished vase, Tim Parsons.

former is too thin it will retain the heat too quickly for it to be dipped and the pewter will just fall back into the pot. Large shallow pieces can also create problems as when dipped the shallowness of the former makes it easier for the pewter to fall straight off.

Pewter cracked? When the pewter cools it may sometimes crack; this can be utilized to become part of the piece.

Slush Casting

Slush casting is a method of casting generally used commercially to produce a hollow form, mainly for items such as door handles, teapot spouts and salt and pepper pots – items that need to be hollow, where only the outside will be seen, or there is a need to minimize the weight of the piece.

The process entails pouring molten pewter into a metal mould, and then before the pewter has solidified pouring it out, so a wall of pewter is left inside the mould. As it requires rapid cooling of the surface, a metal mould is needed for the process to be successful. The mould is usually made in two parts, although sometimes more sections can be used for more complicated pieces. Traditionally the moulds were made of gunmetal or bronze, but brass and aluminium are now also used. As the moulds are very durable it is possible for them to be used thousands of times. Some pewter companies still have moulds that are hundreds of years old.

Although this is probably not a technique employed regularly in a small workshop, it is however still possible to do. The advantage of this method is that there will not be a soldered seam around the main body of the piece.

When choosing a design that will be made using the slush casting technique ensure that, as with making a plaster mould, there are no undercuts, as there is obviously no flexibility in the plaster or the metal. If a plaster two-part mould is made it is possible to take this to a foundry and get it cast in bronze or aluminium to be then used as a slush casting mould.

Once you have the metal mould you need to do some experimenting, and inevitably the first few castings will not be successful as the mould needs to reach the right temperature. If the mould is cold it will not create a smooth finish on the final casting, so sometimes it is worth pouring the pewter into the mould and leaving it to go solid so the mould can heat up.

When the mould is ready it should be coated with a mix of jeweller's rouge and egg white; this coats the mould and has the same role as the talc or graphite powder in other moulds. It should then be clamped together ready for the pewter. The pewter should be heated to approximately 300°C, then poured quickly into the mould; it is impossible to say how long exactly to leave the pewter inside as there are so many possible variables that will affect it, such as the size of the mould, how thick you want the pewter wall to be and the temperature of the pewter. It is worth experimenting with different lengths of time and noting the results for each until the perfect casting is achieved.

Once the piece has been cast it can be finished as appropriate, whether that is soldering on a base or simply cleaning and polishing it. The advantage of this method is that there will not be a soldered seam around the main body of the piece.

EXPERIMENTAL CASTING

Designer **Ian Mcintyre** uses the slush casting technique, but in reverse, to create some unique bowl designs. Using a metal open bowl mould he pours the pewter into the mould, swirls it around the inside of the bowl to form a fine skin, then pours the excess away. This way the outside of the bowl maintains a shiny, smooth finish and the inside captures the movement of the pewter and retains the texture, to create unique designs. This bowl was given as a gift to each of the world leaders present at the G20 Summit in 2009.

Slush cast bowl and process, Ian Mcintyre (photographer Jerry Harman-Jones).

Victoria Brown is a textiles felt artist who has created a range of sculptural pieces by pouring the pewter direct into a felt mould. Using traditional hand felting techniques she makes a two-part felt mould around a glass object, then removes the glass and pours the pewter directly into the mould. Once the pewter has solidified and completely cooled the mould is opened to reveal the pewter. Because the pewter has a low melting point and the felt mould's walls are made quite thick, the pewter singes and carbonizes the area directly around the pewter. This creates an interesting contrast between the pewter and the brightly coloured felt strands of the wool which also become embedded in the pewter, creating an interesting surface texture.

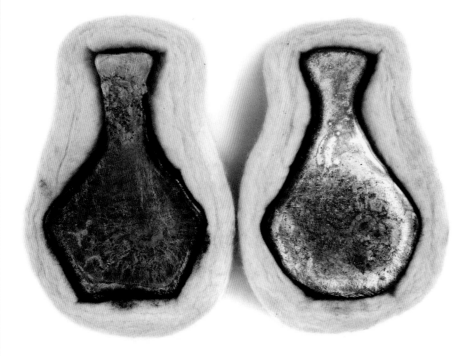

Experimental sculpture: pewter cast into felt, Victoria Brown.

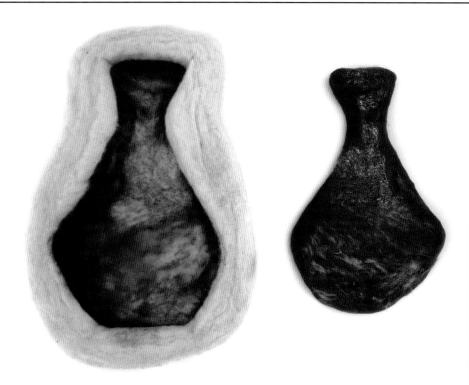

Felt mould and pewter casting, Victoria Brown.

Another interesting technique used by **Tim Parsons** to make his Splash Bowl is to use a steel former in a bowl shape, the negative of the bowl, and drip molten pewter onto it. The pewter cools quickly to produce pools of pewter, which is very smooth on the inside as it is in direct contact with the former and has an uneven texture on the outside. Once the bowl is complete, solder is flooded into the gaps to prevent the bowl separating.

Pewter being dripped onto a steel former, Tim Parsons.

**Pewter Splash Dish,
Tim Parsons.**

Designer **Max Lamb** used a traditional sand casting technique to produce a pewter stool, with a twist. He chose Caerhays beach in Cornwall, as the sand had consistent grain and was free from pebbles and shells, making it possible to carve a precise mould in the sand. He used the side of the beach that was completely below the sea during high tide, so the sand was very well compacted. With simple tools such as a metal rod, a small plant dibber and a kitchen knife, he carved the design into the sand. To melt the pewter he set up a portable twin gas cooker. In experiments he found that the molten pewter did not always reach the bottom of the mould which caused the legs to be differing lengths, so he decided on a three-legged stool which would be stable if the legs were uneven. The seat was created by carving a triangular mesh, which allowed for a larger sitting area and reduced weight, as well as being a more economical use of the pewter. The molten metal was poured first into the legs, filling them all to the same level. Then hotter pewter was added filling the legs and the rest of the seat. As the pewter was still molten they fused together. The pewter cooled in ten minutes, and he dug the shiny stool out of the sand.

Carving the stool design into the sand, Max Lamb.

Pewter poured into the mould, Max Lamb.

Complete cast pewter stool, Max Lamb.

Centrifugal Casting

Unlike gravity casting, where the pewter is simply poured into a static mould, centrifugal casting relies on the force created by a machine that rotates the mould at speed, as the pewter is being poured in through a central pouring hole. The mould rotating creates a centrifugal force that pushes the pewter from the central core along the sprues and into the cavities. Centrifugal casting is ideal for creating small intricate multiple castings in one pouring of pewter.

The centrifugal force being used to push the pewter into the cavities enables very small detailed castings to be made. This is the traditional method for making soldiers and figurines which is also used today. Commercial pewter companies use it on a large scale, but machines are also available that are more suitable for a smaller workshop.

The machine itself is very simple. It comprises a steel box which contains a motor that runs off a standard electricity supply hidden in the bottom section of the box. All that is visible in the bottom of the box is a tri arm that locks the mould in place. The lid has a hole that is positioned directly above the centre of the tri arm. When the mould is locked in place and the lid is closed the tri arm will start to rotate. (A safety feature of this machine ensures that it will only rotate when the lid is closed.)

The machine comes with two mould plates and two mould rings, 17.5cm and 25cm in diameter. There is a set of nylon plugs which are used to create the pouring hole for the pewter and to help the mould sit correctly in the machine. There are also stud clamps and nuts to hold the mould together; these also come in a variety of lengths for making thicker castings. When making a mould for the machine you need the mould plates, nylon plug set, rings and studs to contain the rubber when it is liquid.

The moulds are made in two parts as described previously (see page 46). The rings replace the Lego used with the gravity casting moulds and the mould plates are used instead of a tile. If you are making a thicker casting you need to use the longer length studs and an extra set of rings, to increase the height of the wall.

It is important to remember that when the pewter is poured in through the central reservoir the mould will be rotating in a clockwise direction. This means the centrifugal force within the mould will be in an anticlockwise direction. When setting up patterns to make your mould this should be considered when positioning the patterns. If the pattern is positioned at a slight angle the pewter will flow more easily into the mould;

alternatively if the pattern comes straight from the central core the pewter will be fighting against the centrifugal force.

Consideration should also be given to an even distribution of weight within the mould; an uneven balance of the patterns will stop the turntable from spinning smoothly. Putting smaller, lighter patterns to the outside of the mould is advisable as the lighter patterns will cool quicker. If they are small and on the outside edge they will have a longer sprue but still have time to cool before the sprue has solidified. If the heavier castings are placed nearer to the central reservoir of pewter, they should also have time to fill before the pewter in the sprue cools.

When both halves of the mould have been made it is a good idea to cut a small groove from top to bottom on the outside edge of both parts of the mould; this will help to locate the two halves in the correct position when they have been pulled apart.

When cutting the sprues try to cut from the heaviest part of the pattern as this will solidify after the thinner sections. Using a sprue cutter cut from the pattern and cut lower into the rubber as you move towards the central reservoir; this creates the funnel effect described in previous mould-making sections. Once all the sprues have been cut on the bottom, brush the mould with talc or graphite powder, put the two halves back together and as with the previous mould making where there is no talc this can be cut so the sprues are in the same place on both halves. Then try casting the pewter into the mould.

When casting into the mould, position the machine next to the melting pot to decrease any possibilities of the pewter cooling. Make sure you are wearing a face shield and long arm leather gloves and the lid is closed. It can initially take some practice pouring the pewter into the mould while it is rotating, and to get the correct amount of pewter into the mould without it spilling over the top. Once the pewter starts to pool in the central reservoir stop pouring. Keep the machine on until the pewter in the reservoir has started to solidify. When the pewter has cooled turn off the machine, remove the mould and, with caution in case it is still warm, remove the castings.

The speed can be adjusted between 200 to 900rpm (rotations per minute); larger machines for commercial use will operate to a faster rpm. It is this centrifugal force that forces the pewter into the mould. The general rule is that the small 17.5cm plates will run at a faster speed than that of the larger 25cm one. A faster speed is sometimes needed for some more intricate castings, as the greater the speed the quicker

Centrifugal casting machine, with plates, mould rings
(courtesy of Tiranti).

the pewter is forced into the mould so the pewter retains its heat.

PROBLEMS

Controlling the pewter at higher speeds? If the pewter is poured in too fast it quickly rises up the sides and onto the top of the steel plates, making it very difficult to pull the two halves apart. There are many variables with for example the speed and temperature on each mould as each will have its own characteristics, but a bit of experimenting will soon achieve the right result.

Sprues too small? You may find that for some of the patterns the sprues that have already been cut are sufficient, but if it looks like some will need to be made bigger try not to increase the hole going into the casting too much, as a loss of detail will result. You may want to try casting it a couple of times before doing this so the mould can reach the right temperature, and just the fact that it is a new mould may initially hinder the molten pewter.

An area is constantly not filling? If this happens, it may be that air is becoming trapped; if this is happening it is possible to cut a small vent moving away from the problem area or using a drill (maximum 1mm) you can drill a hole straight through the mould. It may also be that the pattern being cast is a bit more irregular and needs extra sprues going into it. Do not be afraid to try different things.

Thin bits protrude from the edges of the casting? This is called flashing and occurs sometimes when pewter is forced between the two halves of the mould. Small amounts can be removed by running a knife round the edge of the casting and scraping it off. If it happens a lot check the nuts have been put on tightly, or it may be that the speed of the rotations needs to be reduced.

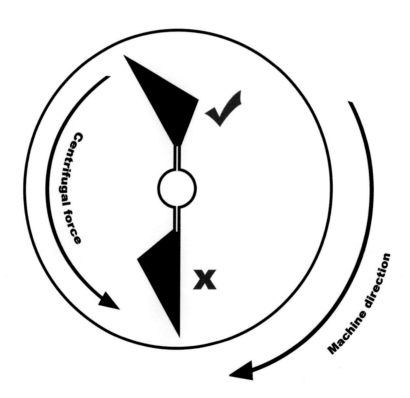

Correct angle for patterns to be positioned in the mould.

EXPERIMENTAL CENTRIFUGAL CASTING

Ammonite bowl and spoon, Glover and Smith.

Pewter and crystal earrings, Gill Clement, in collaboration with A.E. Williams, Birmingham (photographer Raffaella Sirtoli).

This bowl and spoon and the earrings were made using centrifugal casting. One advantage is you can create multiples of one design quickly, which is why it is one of the main production methods in commercially produced pewter.

It is still possible however to create unique individual designs using this method, such as this blossom centrepiece. I made the main part from four elements. Actual twigs were used as the pattern. The twigs were put in hot water initially, then put between two heavy flat surfaces so they would dry quite flat, enabling the mould to be thinner, so using less rubber. Three flowers were modelled in Milliput. One mould was made that contained all of these elements, so that one pour would create all the sections needed, excluding the base.

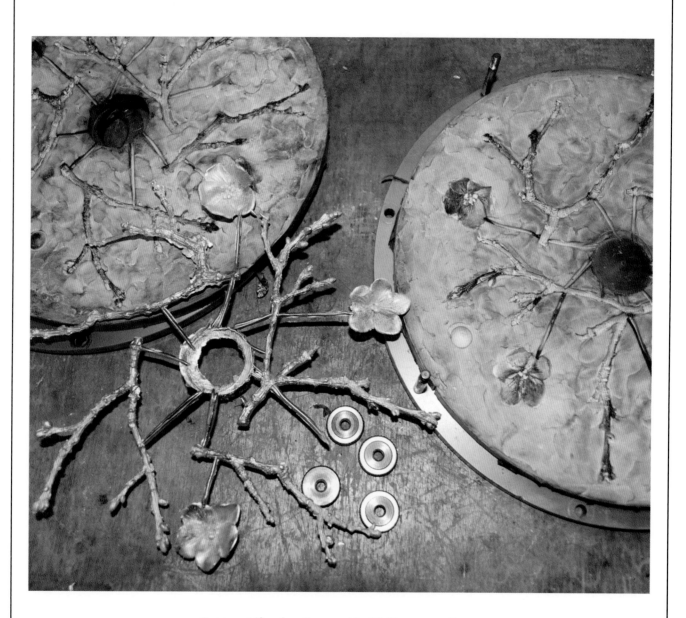

Open centrifugal casting mould with blossom castings.

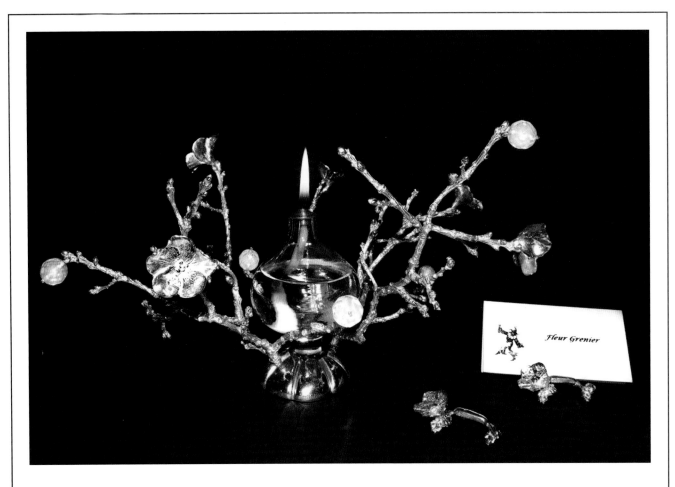

Blossom centrepiece, author.

Once the pieces had been cast the sprues were cut off with flat end cutters, any flashing was removed, and all the pieces were put into a barrel polisher.

When the castings were all polished each twig was carefully bent using my hands to get back the original three-dimensional look and then all the pieces were soldered together onto the base, including the flowers. Because there are possibilities for them to be soldered in lots of different ways each centrepiece can be different.

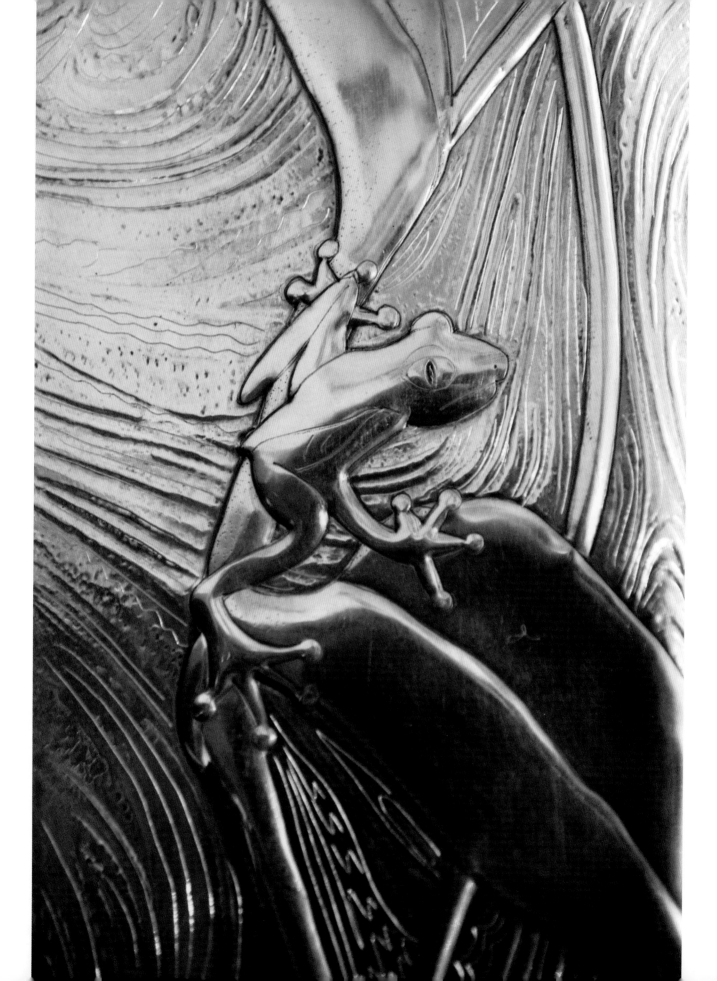

SURFACE DECORATION

Repoussé blanks.

REPOUSSÉ

Repoussé (from *pousser* the French verb for 'push') is a method of creating a pattern on the surface of a very thin sheet of metal using rounded tools to raise sections and create intricate details in the pewter. It is a technique that can be started with very little equipment and can be as simple or as complicated as you would like it to be. Once the skill has been developed beautiful intricate designs can be produced. The

OPPOSITE PAGE:
Mirror by Bonnie Macintosh (detail).

pewter used is very thin sheet, usually about 0.15mm thick, the designs are worked on from the front and the back creating high and low relief designs.

As the pewter sheet used is so thin it is too soft to support itself for most designs. That is why blanks are used. A blank is an object, such as a box, picture frame or piece of jewellery, that the pewter is applied to, to give the pewter support and structure. It is possible to buy some ready-made blanks or you can make your own. Most blanks bought in hobby shops are made very simply in plywood or aluminium, as the pewter will be covering most if not all of it so a good finish is not essential. Some designers such as Bonnie Macintosh and Marai Santos make the blank an integral part of the design so it needs to be of a high standard to complete the overall look of the piece. Engaging with craftsmen that work in these areas can ensure they are well made.

It is useful to examine some pieces, comparing the initial blank and the final design. Used by **Partners in Pewter** some of these blanks were bought, such as the brooch backs, picture frame, box and coasters. Others were made to order, like the blank for the spun pewter wine bottle stand. The technique can be used for a wide variety of designs ranging from simple book covers to mirrors and tables.

Sue Rawley creates a wide range of designs using the *repoussé* technique, ranging from small hand mirrors and band boxes to wall panels and mirrors. She designs and commissions pieces to be made to use as a base for her *repoussé* work such as the six-sided pedestal. This piece was influenced by the Moorish art from the Alhambra Palace, the whole piece is decorated with fine intricate details and large slices of agate and lapis that are highlighted when they are lit up from inside the pedestal, creating a rich, lavish piece. She is influenced by many sources for her work – medieval art, Arts and Crafts, boxes which were used by the Byzantine, precious oils, botanical influences such as magnified seed heads, dragon flies and moths – all of which you will find if you look closely at her work.

Other *repoussé* artists make the base-object an important part of the piece. **Bonnie Macintosh** commissions glass pieces to be made, then uses them as an integral part of the design and creates the piece around them. For these pieces sections of *repoussé* are carefully cut out and adhered to the glass, creating a beautiful contrasting design, not only with the colour but by juxtaposing the simplicity of the glass with the intricate detailing of the pewter.

Six-sided pedestal, Sue Rawley.

Glass and *Repoussé* vase, Bonnie Macintosh (photography FXP).

Fallen Trees box, Maria Santos.

Detail of Dragon Fire screen, Adrian and Lesley Doble.

Repoussé requires a great deal of skill, control, sensitivity and understanding of the pewter. It is possible to make very simple designs and shapes, but a well-executed design can take a great deal of time, with each mark being made by hand, working from the back and the front of the pewter. To achieve a perfect finish is very time consuming, but beautiful pieces can be created, as can be seen in these examples of work by **Maria Santos**, and **Adrian and Lesley Doble.**

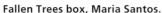

Repoussé tools.

EXERCISE

Making a Brooch

EQUIPMENT

- Brooch blank
- Piece of pewter foil 0.15mm thick
- Permanent pen
- Pencil
- Tracing paper and cartridge paper
- Smooth hard board or work surface
- Piece of leather, soft cloth or felt
- Selection of modelling tools (wooden clay modelling tools are ideal as they come in a wide variety of shapes and sizes and will not scratch the pewter, also ball tools, leather making tools, old ball point pens and tracing and burnishing tools)
- Polyfilla (it does not need to be ready mixed but that can be easier to use, and as only small quantities are used it is not very expensive)
- Ruler
- Craft knife
- Evostick, Pritt stick
- Small pair of sharp scissors
- Cotton wool
- Rubber or latex gloves
- Acetone/methylated spirits
- Metal cleaner (such as Brasso)
- Blackening solution

This is a simple exercise to become familiar with the repoussé tools and techniques. A letter was chosen for the design, as it has to be worked from the back and the front of the pewter, so showing a variety of techniques.

Choose a blank for the brooch. These are usually made from aluminium with a pin stuck on the back. They can be bought pre-made or you can make your own. For this initial project it is better to select a simple shape: round, square or oval.

Select your letter: this can be a simple printout from the computer. Make it a size that will fit neatly onto the blank with extra space around it to texture the background.

With a permanent pen draw round the blank on the pewter. Using a pencil draw round the blank on the tracing paper. Position the tracing paper over the letter paper printout with the letter in the middle of the circle. Match the circles drawn on the tracing paper and on the pewter, remembering to position it so the letter is back to front, as we initially work from the back of the brooch. Trace the line onto the pewter, and when you have drawn all the way around remove the paper and go over the line again to make it more defined.

Lay down a piece of leather or soft cloth to provide a soft surface to work on when using the repousse tools to create an impression in the pewter.

Turn the pewter over to the front, then using a wooden tracing tool draw all around the outside edge of the letter; this gives the letter more definition.

Turning the sheet over again so you are working from the back, using a flat wooden tool start at one side of the

Raising the letter, from the back.

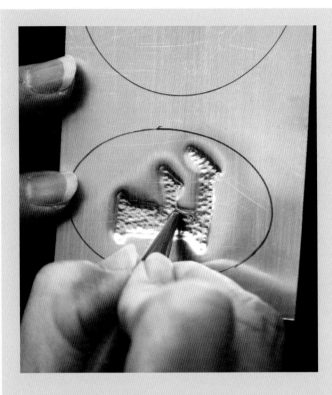

Raising the letter, creating a stippled effect.

RAISING HIGH AND LOW PATTERNS

When you become more familiar with the repoussé technique and start to produce more complicated designs, it is important to remember that all the lower relief areas should be done first, as if you start with the higher areas they will get damaged and squashed if you then move onto the lower areas. If doing a complicated design, plan the different levels beforehand, starting with the lowest level, and indicate them on the pewter sheet with numbers from 1 upwards. This will help you to remember the different stages without any of the areas becoming squashed.

Once the letter is complete it will need to be filled so that it does not get damaged. Put some of the Polyfilla onto a knife or a scraper and push the filler into the hollow, slowly moving it across until it is full and has a flat even surface. It can then be left to completely dry or a hairdryer can speed up the process.

When the filler is completely dry the excess can be removed with a damp cloth. Any stubborn filler can be removed with the scraper or your fingernail, being careful not to make grooves and dents in the metal. All the excess should be removed, as they will show through on the surface of the brooch as lumps, which can ruin the final design.

inside of the letter and then with even pressure move the tool across to the opposite line. It is important to work in lines directly from one side to the other; otherwise stopping and starting can create a lumpy uneven surface.

Once the whole letter has been done turn the pewter over and using the wooden tracing tool go around the outside of the letter to give a sharper edge. To increase the depth turn over to the front and repeat the process.

Because the metal is supported by the leather, which is soft, the pewter can be stretched without being restrained by a hard surface. It is possible to increase the depth by folding the leather to increase its thickness, and then repeat the process. There are limitations as the metal is very thin and it will reach a point where it becomes too fatigued and weak, so the tool just pierces straight through the pewter.

Another method of raising the surface is to use a small ball-ended tool, and moving around the inside of the letter, push into the pewter creating a stippled effect that also raises the height of the letter. Work all over the letter to create an even height; then as done previously turn the pewter over and trace around the outside edge to give the letter more definition.

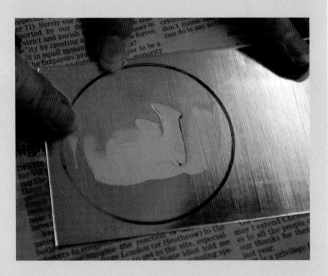

Filling the raised area with Polyfilla.

If the filler is not completely dry the cloth may drag some of it out of the hollow or alternatively sometimes as the filler dries it shrinks. Either way it is important that the filler sits flush with the surface of the pewter so more should be added until it is completely flat.

If the pewter is being attached to a shaped or rounded object, when the damp cloth has been used to clean up the surface this dampens the filler again, so this is an ideal time to shape the pewter so the filler does not crack and fall out. Use the object, for example a cylinder, and carefully move the pewter around it, then leave to dry completely.

While the filler is drying the blank can be prepared. Cover the surface of the blank with glue such as Pritt stick, then push firmly onto a piece of cartridge paper (the thicker the paper the deeper the impressions on the pewter will be). Once the paper is in place cut neatly all around the edge of the disc. Then using a nailfile or a piece of coarse sandpaper go round the edge of the blank to make it as neat as possible.

When complete rub more glue onto the surface of the paper and, using the line previously drawn around your letter, position the blank centrally on your pewter sheet, making sure the letter is the correct way up in relation to the pin. Then using your hands gently squeeze together.

Using a pair of sharp scissors cut all around the edge of the blank leaving an approximate 3mm border. It really

MAKING A NEAT BACK

You can neaten the back so the blank cannot be seen at all. Making sure the pin is closed, gently press the back of the brooch into a piece of pewter sheet that is large enough to cover the back. This will create two indents at the two ends of the brooch. Using a leather punch make two holes in the marked spots. Open the pin and position the pewter onto the back. The holes may need to be adjusted to allow for the pin, particularly the hinged end. It is better to make all the adjustments prior to putting the glue on, as it can get very messy if the pewter is being lifted on and off.

Once it fits neatly, if you would like to make patterns on the back as well this can be done before gluing it in place. Remove any lumps of dry glue from the back then put a thin layer of glue all around the edge, using your fingers gently squeeze together and then using the scissors neatly cut up to the edge. This will create a sharp edge that will need to be removed so again using the burnisher rub the edge until such a neat edge has been created that it is difficult to see the seam. This is where it is also important to make sure all the Polyfilla has been removed as the smallest amount will be highlighted becoming a raised lump in the pewter.

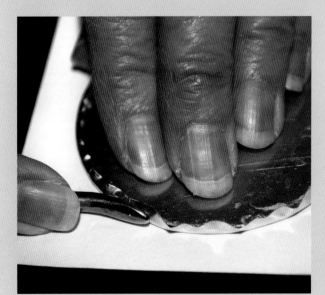

Folding and burnishing the edge of the brooch.

Punching the holes to go over the brooch mechanism on the back.

does not want to be any larger than this; there should be enough to fold over the edge of the blank and a little bit to burnish over the back surface – too much and it makes it very difficult to rub over neatly as lots of creases and folds start to form.

Once the full circle is cut, put a thin layer of Evostick all around the edge of the blank. Slowly start to fold the pewter. Try to get the fold as close as possible to the edge of the blank; it is better to work around doing a bit at a time until all the edge is completely folded over. Using a bent tracing or burnishing tool gently rub around the perimeter and over the back surface. This will force out any excess glue. Continue with this until the side and back is completely smooth.

Once the edges have all been burnished the front is ready to be finished. If you are going to be making a few brooches a simple tool that can be very useful is a piece of wood with a central grove cut out. The pin sits neatly in the groove enabling you to get even pressure over the piece without it moving around. While working like this if you find it puts strain on your wrist you may want to roll up some of the leather or a soft cloth and position it under your wrist; this will give you support and steady your hand while working.

As the paper has been glued under the pewter it allows the metal to stretch as it acts as a cushion; if the pewter was glued directly onto the blank the tools would just scratch the surface.

You may want to practise various texturing effects with different tools before moving onto the actual piece. If the letter has been created using the stippling effect you might want to keep the background quite simple so it does not become lost.

Once the texturing has been completed the brooch is ready to be finished. There may be some grease on the surface; this can be caused by the rollers that were used to roll the sheet initially and by handling, and must be removed prior to polishing. Wearing gloves to stop any irritation to your hands, put some acetone on a piece of cotton wool and gently wipe across the surface.

When all the dirt has been removed take a soft duster and put a small amount of liquid metal polisher on it, then gently rub across the piece in one direction for a couple of minutes. (Coarser polish such as Brasso should be used, as the silver polishes are too fine to remove any of the patinated finish.) With a clean duster remove the polish. You should be left with a highly polished surface.

To highlight the patterned areas more, brush the surface with blackening solution until an evenly finished surface appears. Once the brooch is completely black rinse off the solution, dry and repeat the polishing process. As the cloth will not reach into the smaller details these areas are left dark, making a greater contrast with the polished sections.

The brooch is now ready to be worn.

Starting to create a patterned background.

Completed brooches.

ETCHING

The etching process is also used to create patterns and textures on the surface of the metal. Unlike the *repoussé* however, where the metal is manipulated with tools, etching uses an acid to physically remove the metal from areas that are left unprotected.

There are various types of etching such as acid etching, photo etching and laser etching. Acid etching uses a chemical solution. The typical acids used for etching pewter are ferric chloride, ferric nitrate or nitric acid.

Photo etching treats the surface of the metal with a photosensitive coating; the pattern/design is put onto a photo resist sheet; this sheet is then transferred onto the metal using an ultra violet light. When the metal is chemically treated the photo resist areas then act as a barrier. Very detailed pieces can be made in this way.

The process of laser etching, cutting and engraving uses a laser, usually operated by a computer, to cut and engrave the metal. This is a very clean process ideal for large production runs, but it can also be used for one-off designs.

Acid Etching

The most practical and simple etching process to set up in a small scale workshop is acid etching. You need very little equipment to produce detailed results. Unlike other metals such as copper and silver, pewter takes longer to etch, because the main alloy, tin, is not as susceptible to attack from the acid as other metals.

Ferric chloride acid etching set-up.

You can create the most basic etching set-up and can produce excellent results with a glass or plastic container large enough to hold the work so it can sit comfortably in the acid and attain an even etch. Never use a metal container.

You can buy a bubble tank specially made for etching. If you will be doing a lot of etching it may be worth considering buying one for the workshop. The tank works by maintaining the acid at an even temperature; this can speed up the etching process. The pewter is suspended in a cage in the tank which enables the bubbles to circulate around the metal so the acid eats into the pewter and the residue falls away from the metal rather than resting on the surface and causing an obstruction and slowing down the process.

It is possible to make your own simple version of a bubble tank with a small fish tank pump set up in the glass dish so it circulates the air. The acid is gently heated by placing the acid bath within another bowl of boiling water, which is usually enough for ferric chloride, nitric or ferric nitrate.

If it will not harm the work, drill a hole in the pewter so a length of wire can be put through so it can be suspended into the dish. Alternatively a piece of wire longer than the width of the bowl can be taped onto the back using a strong tape, then the two ends folded over the sides of the bowl. Suspending the pewter in acid causes the etched residue to fall away from the piece. Both these tanks will speed up the etching process.

Care should be taken that the solution is not too warm as it will make the solution more aggressive and possibly lose some detail.

When making your own bubble tank, if the dish being used is quite small the pump may be too strong, making the etch very aggressive. This can result in a lot of detail being lost and the lines losing their sharpness. Putting a clip on the tube forcing the air into the dish will restrict the airflow making the bubbles more gentle and resulting in a neater etch. When positioning the work in the tank try not to position it directly in front of the tube releasing the bubbles as this can create an uneven etch.

Acids

There are several acids that can be used to etch the pewter. Ferric chloride, ferric nitrate and nitric acid will each have different working times. When working with any of them it is important to remember health and safety issues.

and cooling it will slow it down; the warmer and stronger the solution the rougher the etched surface will be.

When etching with acid always start with the etched areas polished very smooth and clean.

FERRIC CHLORIDE

Ferric chloride is probably the most non-toxic solution to use. It gives off non-toxic vapours and causes little hazard if used occasionally and if it comes in contact with skin. This does not mean however that safety precautions should not be observed.

Ferric chloride has the advantage that it is inexpensive and is readily available either ready mixed or as crystals for mixing. It is quite a messy acid to work with – it is important to note that it will stain anything it comes in contact with so it is worth covering the area you will be working in.

If only doing a small amount of etching ferric chloride is the most readily available acid as it can be bought from high street electrical shops where it is sold as a copper etchant for making circuit boards. It is available in packets that are ready to be mixed with water. Or if you are doing a lot of etching most chemical suppliers will have it in stock.

When the ferric chloride solution is active it is a cloudy brown colour, but when it has been used and becomes exhausted it turns a translucent blue. When it has turned this colour it will no longer etch the metal and should be disposed of. Contact your local hazardous waste for disposal, or it can be neutralized with sodium carbonate (washing soda).

If etching with ferric chloride it is advisable to work with the chloride when it is warm, no warmer than 55°C. One way to maintain this temperature is to place your container of acid inside another bowl of hot water; this helps to warm the solution.

A quite shallow etch can be achieved by leaving the pewter in the solution for about 20 minutes. For a deeper etch it should be left 1–2 hours. These times are dependent upon the strength of the acid and the temperature so should only be used as a guideline.

NITRIC ACID

Nitric acid will etch quicker than ferric chloride or ferric nitrate. It is possible to achieve a shallow etch in 4–5 minutes and quite a deep etch after about 20 minutes, if the solution is gently warmed as done with the ferric chloride. If using a cold solution it will take a little longer.

For your safety…

WORKING WITH ACID

When working with any of these acids, always wear safety glasses, rubber gloves, facemask and plastic apron to protect against splashing.

If any acid does splash, rinse skin thoroughly. If splashed in the eye rinse thoroughly for five minutes, then consult a doctor.

FERRIC CHLORIDE

Relatively harmless, but still rinse immediately if splashed.

Cover the area you will be working in, to avoid staining.

NITRIC ACID

Add the acid to the water and not the other way round, in case it splashes.

Do not overheat nitric acid, as it will release harmful fumes.

Ensure sufficient ventilation to draw away any harmful fumes.

If storing any nitric acid ensure that it is clearly labelled. In a shared workshop keep in a locked cabinet.

To dispose of any used nitric acid contact your local hazardous waste department.

FERRIC NITRATE

Rinse thoroughly and wash with a non-abrasive soap if ferric nitrate comes in contact with skin.

Protect the working area, as it can be a messy acid to work with.

To dispose of any used ferric nitrate contact your local hazardous waste department.

As well as the acids having different working times, varying the way the acid is prepared can also alter the etching times. A stronger solution will speed up the process, but it may also affect the etched finish, as a stronger acid will etch thicker lines and start to undercut the resist whereas a weaker solution will create a fine line and will etch straight down producing a neater finish. The temperature of the acid is also a consideration. Warming the acid will speed up the process

Although the nitric will work faster than the other acids it does have some disadvantages in that it has a lot more health and safety considerations. It is also more expensive and not as readily available.

Nitric acid can be used again as long as it has been stored correctly in an airtight container.

The proportion is one part acid to four parts water. When mixing the solution it is very important that the acid is added to the water and not the other way round in case it splashes. If overheated, it will release harmful fumes. Only work with nitric acid in an area that has sufficient ventilation to draw away any harmful fumes. If storing any nitric acid label it clearly and put in a locked cabinet if in a shared workshop. To dispose of any used nitric acid contact your local hazardous waste department.

FERRIC NITRATE

Ferric nitrate is very similar to ferric chloride in appearance and in the results it achieves. The results in terms of etching times are also very similar. A shallow etch can be achieved in about 20 minutes and a deeper etch in 1–2 hours. The one difference is that the etched areas seem to have a rougher surface than that of the ferric chloride or nitric acid. This is not noticeable in very fine etching but seems more pronounced on larger areas that are polished after etching. This can however be used as an advantage to create a contrast between the etched and the smooth, untouched pewter.

Like the ferric chloride it can be a messy acid to work with so all the working area should be protected. As with the other acids, wear safety goggles, rubber gloves and plastic apron. If the ferric nitrate comes in contact with skin it should be rinsed thoroughly and washed with a non-abrasive soap. To dispose of it contact your local hazardous waste department.

Protecting Areas with a Resist

In order to etch the pewter a design must first be transferred onto the metal. A 'resist' is used so that only the areas without the resist will be removed by the acid. There is a wide variety of materials that can be used, such as:

RHIND'S STOPPING OUT VARNISH

This is normally used as part of the printing process. It is a white spirit-based brown varnish that can be brushed onto the metal and left to dry. You can paint areas quite accurately with a fine brush. You can also work in reverse, painting the whole area, then using tracing paper transfer a design onto it. The varnish can then be removed in the relevant areas with a scriber or pointed wax carving tools. If the varnish becomes too thick a small amount of white spirit can be added and stirred in thoroughly to make it thinner.

The Circle Etched Bowl was made using a stop-out. The whole of the top of the bowl was painted, and the design

Ferric nitrate and ferric chloride samples; nitrate surface is coarser.

Stamped and etched Circle Bowl, author.

was scratched using circle templates and wax tools to remove the varnish. As the bowl had a dip in the centre, rather than immersing the whole bowl in the acid, which would have required a lot of acid, a small plasticine wall was built around the top edge of the bowl as a precaution to stop any spilling down the sides. Then the hollow was filled with the acid. After the piece was etched white spirit was used to remove the varnish.

Wax

Candle wax or beeswax can be dripped onto the surface to create some interesting splash effects. It can also be melted and brushed onto the surface and then cut into to remove sections, but it is quite difficult to create fine details using the brushed-on technique. To remove the wax use hot soapy water. Pour it onto the surface of the metal over a bowl half-filled with cold water. The wax solidifies when it comes in contact with the cold water and can be easily removed and thrown away. Do not pour it down the drain with the water, as it can block the drains.

Dalo Etch Resist Marker Pen

This pen is used for marking electronic circuit boards. To fill the tip with the resist put slight pressure onto the tip. This forces the nib to retract into the pen and the tip is then refreshed with the resist. This pen is ideal for drawing with or patching up areas. If you want to create a deep etch you may need to build up layers. To remove use white spirit.

Permanent Pen

Any everyday permanent pen is ideal for using with ferric chloride and ferric nitrate, as it adheres to the surface and is resistant to the acid. It is not suitable for creating a deep etched design as it can wear away. The advantage of using these pens is that they are readily available and can be bought with various size tips.

Photocopy on Acetate

A pattern is copied onto acetate and this is then transferred onto the pewter using a domestic iron. This is ideal for creating intricate patterns on the surface such as this Leaf Cutter Ant box. A colour photograph of some leaf cutter ants was changed on the computer to black and white, giving it strong contrast. It was printed onto paper, then copied onto acetate. The design was transferred onto a flat piece of pewter, etched and then fly-pressed to give it the shape. The pewter needs to be flat for the iron to transfer the design evenly onto the metal. (To remove use white spirit.)

Etched Leaf Cutter Ant Box, author.

Transferring ant picture from the acetate.

Fablon and Sticky Back Plastic
Designs can be drawn onto the plastic, cut out and transferred onto the pewter. Make sure that you rub over the whole surface with your fingers, forcing out any air bubbles and ensuring it has adhered to the surface. This is really only suitable for a flat area or if doing small areas on a shaped piece where the design can be applied without creasing. Care should be taken if using in a bubble tank as the bubbles can lift the plastic off. (To remove, peel off.)

Stickers
With the growing market in making cards there is now a huge selection of stickers with letters, numbers, patterns and so on. They are produced in small sheets and can be bought in most craft shops. You simply peel the sticker off the sheet and transfer it onto the pewter. It is a quick way to produce neat lettering and numbers. Again it is not suitable for a bubble tank as it can cause the stickers to lift. (To remove peel off.)

Other everyday household products that can be used are Tipp-ex, nail varnish, sellotape, masking tape, in fact most tapes can be used and are good for masking off larger areas such as the back of the piece that is being etched.

Using a Resist

Before using any of these resists remember the surface of the metal should be clean of grease so there is nothing creating a barrier between the two. It is also important to put a resist around the edge of the piece of pewter, or the acid will eat

through, creating undercuts. The Dalo pen is useful for this as it is easy to use to draw all around the edge.

If possible it is better to give the pewter an initial polish prior to etching, as once the piece is etched if it is then polished the mops may remove some of the detail. If the piece is given a final polish with a swansdown mop and rouge, once it has been etched it will not be too abrasive. Remember to wash with hot soapy water to remove the polishing compound before etching as this will act as a resist.

When the pewter has been in the acid the area that has been etched will be a dark grey, which highlights the contrasts in the designs. If there are larger areas that have been etched and the piece is then given a final polish the mop will make these areas polished too, but the grey near to the edge of the line will remain where the mop cannot reach, so still creating a contrast. This can be seen on the Circle Bowl (*see* page 83).

EXERCISE

Etch a Set of Coasters

This exercise is to produce a set of four coasters. Four methods of etching will be described: using stickers, acetate, varnish and wax. This means each coaster could be different, or you may chose to use just one method and produce a matching set.

MAKING THE COASTERS

EQUIPMENT

- 4 pieces of pewter 1.5–2mm thick and approximately 9.5cm x 9.5cm and
- Piercing saw
- File
- Emery stick with 400 emery paper
- Wide tape (parcel tape or duct tape)

Decide what shape you would like the coaster to be; it could be geometric or an organic shape. You may chose to have four the same or all different. Work out the design and transfer it onto the pewter. Then using a piercing saw cut out all four shapes. Once they have been cut out neaten up the edges with a file. Then use an emery stick with 400 emery paper to remove all the file marks and burrs.

Using a polishing motor polish each piece front and back so the surface is free from any marks and scratches. Then wash thoroughly with hot soapy water to remove any grease. Once they have been washed try to avoid touching the surface and leaving any greasy fingerprints.

To protect the back of the coasters from the acid apply a wide tape such as parcel tape or duct tape on the back, carefully rubbing all over the surface to make sure there are no air bubbles for the acid to leak through. Then remove the excess tape using scissors.

PREPARING THE PATTERN FOR ETCHING

COASTER 1: STICKERS

EQUIPMENT

- Polished pewter coaster
- Stickers
- Craft knife
- Dalo pen/permanent pen

This is the simplest method of making a design. Select the stickers you would like to use. Lift them off the sheet

Coaster and stickers.

with a craft knife to stop any grease from your fingers going onto the adhesive part of the sticker or the pewter. Position them on the coaster

Using a soft cloth gently rub over the surface of each sticker to ensure it is securely stuck to the pewter. Then using the Dalo or permanent pen mark around the outside edge of the coaster. You may also want to use the pen to do additional patterns on the surface or create border around the edge of the surface of the coaster. The coaster is now ready to be etched.

COASTER 2: STOP-OUT VARNISH

EQUIPMENT

- Polished pewter coaster
- Rhind's Stopping Out Varnish
- Paintbrush
- Tracing paper
- Metal scriber or pointed wax carving tool

Paint an even coat of the varnish all over the surface and the outside edge of the coaster and leave to dry. If only a thin layer it will be dry in a few hours, but if thicker if possible leave overnight to ensure it is completely dry.

Work out the design you would like transferred onto the coaster. Mark this out on tracing paper. Rub chalk over the back of the tracing paper, then place it in posi-

Making pattern in the stop-out.

If by mistake you go over the line that you have marked, wait until the varnish is dry, then using the scriber neaten it up until it is back within the marked area. Once it is dry you may also like to add fine detail that could not be achieved with the brush using the scriber. When you are happy that the design is complete it is ready to be etched.

COASTER 3: WAX

EQUIPMENT

■ Polished pewter coaster
■ Wax candle
■ Tape
■ Dalo pen/permanent pen
■ Newspaper

You can use the wax as a resist, as described previously, by melting it and brushing it onto the surface and again transferring a design onto the surface using tracing paper. A simple way that creates an interesting effect is to light the candle, then as the wax melts drip or flick it onto the pewter. Before doing this place several pieces of newspaper on the floor and place the pewter on top; this way you can vary the height more, which also alters the splash effect of the wax.

You can experiment on a piece of dark paper to see how to create different effects. To create a contrast areas can be marked off using the stop-out varnish or tape before using the wax. If you want to remove a small section of wax it can be scratched off using a knife. Once happy with the design it is ready to be etched.

tion on the coaster with the chalk side against the varnish. Using a pencil follow the line of your design until you have gone over the whole design. (Slowly lift off one corner to check that a chalk imprint has been left.) Lift the paper completely and using the scribe follow the chalk line, removing the varnish.

The complete pattern should now be transferred to the coaster. You will now need to work out which areas of the varnish you would like to remove, remembering that where the varnish is left will be the high points. Then using the tools remove the varnish, trying to ensure all of it is removed, as if any is left the acid will etch around it and this could alter the design. Once complete the coaster is ready to be etched.

If the design you have done has more of the pewter etched away, it would be impractical to paint the whole piece. If this is the case mark your design on a piece of tracing paper, then using a soft pencil rub over the back of the tracing paper. Rub a wax candle over the surface of the coaster so you have an even thin layer. Position the design over the pewter with the roughly rubbed pencil side face to face with the pewter. Using a pencil follow the line of the design as done previously. When complete lift the paper; there should be an imprint of the pattern in the wax. Using the scriber follow the line on the pewter. The wax will then need to be removed as this will act a barrier to the acid. Wash thoroughly with hot soapy water until it is all removed. Dry it with a soft cloth, then using the brush paint the varnish onto the areas required.

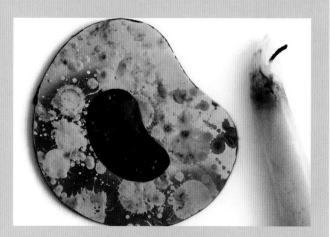

Wax dripped onto the coaster.

COASTER 4: PRINTED ACETATE

EQUIPMENT

■ Polished coaster
■ Laser printed acetate sheet
■ Paper
■ Domestic iron

Select an image or a design, ensuring that there is definite black and white contrast. If using a photograph the image can be manipulated on a computer quite easily in most photo editing programs to ensure a strong difference between black and white. Print the image in black and white. Any grey areas will also transfer and act as a resist, so check this will not ruin the effect of your design.

The photograph is then copied onto acetate using a professional laser copier, which uses heat to adhere the ink to the surface; it is this process that then allows the heat from the iron to transfer the design onto the pewter.

Place the clean pewter on a completely flat surface. Then position the acetate on top with the toner side face down on the metal, and put a piece of paper over the acetate. Using the iron set at a high heat place it on the paper for several minutes. At regular intervals check by lifting the corner of the acetate to see if it has transferred to the metal; if it has not replace the iron and hold down for a bit longer.

Transferring the pattern from the acetate onto the pewter.

The time the iron is held can vary depending on different factors such as the type of pattern being transferred, the pressure of the iron, and how long ago the acetate copy was done. When the pattern has transferred completely to the metal slowly remove the acetate, being careful not to touch the pewter as it will have become very hot. The coaster is ready to etch.

ETCHING THE COASTERS

EQUIPMENT

■ Ferric chloride acid bath
■ Newspaper to protect surface
■ Safety glasses, gloves and apron
■ Coasters prepared with design
■ Plastic tweezers
■ Feather

To keep the exercise simple we are using the basic etch set-up without a pump: a glass or plastic dish (not metal) that is large enough to hold the four coasters flat in the bottom, mixing enough of the ferric chloride to cover the bottom and the coasters, and place the bowl with the acid inside another bowl of hot water to help to keep the acid solution warm; this can be changed at regular intervals if the etching is being left several hours.

Firstly lay newspaper on the work surface to protect the bench from splashes. It is advisable to set up the bath near running water; if this is not possible have a bowl of water nearby so the pieces can be rinsed and you are not carrying work dripping with acid around the workshop. If the bowl is large enough all four coasters should all sit flat on the bottom. Otherwise you can tape a piece of wire to the back of each coaster and suspend them in the bowl so they are immersed in the acid but not touching the bottom. This method enables any of the residue to fall away from the etching.

Before working with the acid, make sure you are wearing safety glasses, gloves and apron. If the coasters are placed directly in the bottom of the bowl, at regular intervals agitate the acid with a feather, lightly brushing over each coaster to remove any air bubbles and etching residue.

Check the pieces regularly to see how the etch is progressing. This can be done by removing one of the coasters with a pair of plastic tweezers, rinsing it thoroughly under a running tap and with a fingernail checking the depth of the etch; if it is still not deep enough place it back into the acid. If the feather does not remove all the residue, remove the pieces from the acid and with a soft brush or sponge remove the excess residue, and the bare metal will start to show through. This can speed up the etch. Check the coasters every half hour. The acetate transfer coaster is not as durable as some of the other resist methods so this coaster will probably need to be removed first.

After approximately two hours the other coasters should have reached a good depth; however if you prefer it to be deeper leave it in the acid longer. There is no definite timescale due to the many factors that can affect it: temperature, strength of the acid, and how often the solution was agitated. The important thing is to keep checking regularly.

Once the etching has reached the desired depth remove the resists as described previously (*see* page 83). Rinse the coasters thoroughly with hot soapy water and a soft sponge; this will help to gently remove any residue left in the etched areas. Then dry them thoroughly with a soft cloth. Check the edges of the coasters; sometimes they may need to be emeryed slightly to create a crisp line.

Once satisfied they are all right you will need to give them a final polish. To finish them properly, so they do not mark surfaces when they are being used, use sticky-back felt sheet that can be cut to size and stuck on.

Completed coasters.

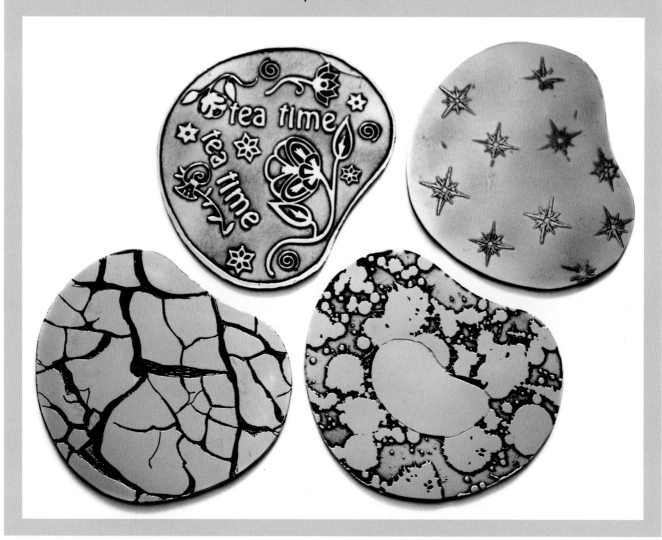

**Etched pewter and glass vase:
pattern created by dripped
wax onto the pewter; the
pewter was then stamped to
create the form, author.**

HAMMERED TEXTURE

A wide range of surface finishes can be achieved with a
hammer alone, ranging from the quite traditional pewter
pattern of a circular indent finish to more intricate linear
finishes. The simple circular indent finish not only creates an
interesting surface texture but creates a different effect as the
light reflects off the piece. It is possible to use the rounded
end of a ball pein hammer – the surface of the hammer should
not be marked, as each strike of the hammer will transfer that
mark onto each hammered dimple on the piece. If there are
marks on the hammer they can be emeryed and polished
out; it is advisable to polish the hammerhead, as you will
guarantee a clean mark on the pewter.

When starting to hammer a texture onto a piece it
should be supported on a hard surface, if a flat piece on the
worktop, or if shaped use an appropriate stake. Different size
indents can be created with different size hammer heads;
blocking hammers used for silversmithing are ideal as they
come in various sizes and weights so different indents can be
created.

Light blows are all that is needed to create the texture,
using short, sharp and swift strikes with the hammer. Different
finishes can be achieved not only with the size of the hammer
head but the weight of it and the force at which each blow is
carried out.

To create a textured pattern, you can use a file to make
lines in the surface of an old hammer face; these lines will

He uses punches for finishing a number of his pewter vessels, with the added difficulty that the double skinned vessels are hollow so extreme care is needed. As this is the final process for the piece, a lot of work and time can be sacrificed for nothing if mistakes are made. For his vessels he

Creating the traditional pewter hammered finish.

Double skinned pewter bowl, Keith Tyssen.

then transfer onto the pewter. It is advisable to experiment on a scrap piece of pewter before moving on to the actual piece. Second-hand tool shops are always a good source of old and unusual hammers. Steel punches and nails can also be used to create a variety of patterns and textures.

Keith Tyssen is an award-winning silversmith/pewtersmith who has been producing beautifully crafted pewter work for a number of years. Since his student days, he has considered pewter an undeservedly sidelined material. Lead-free modern pewter offers many special qualities deserving of a more sophisticated visual design and manufacturing approach, and he has devoted much time to producing a series of carefully considered pewter vessels. The success of his pewterware is that he develops designs that are considerate to the material's metallurgical and visual properties. Each piece is carefully produced from the initial design development and the making of the piece to the final finishing of the object. This great attention to detail results in some beautiful tactile pewter pieces that he has now become so well known for producing.

Creating the riveted pattern around the bowl, Keith Tyssen.

selects the correct tools then works slowly and methodically around the bowl. To disguise the seam he uses several tools to create the effect that the piece is riveted.

When preparing ensure all the tools are to hand and the piece is supported in a way that it will not become scratched or move easily. Also sit in a position that you will be able to work comfortably.

Quick sharp blows are used, controlling the pressure of the strike. Many people using this technique say if possible not to stop part way through, for example if a stippled line was being produced around the edge of a piece. If stopped half way, when the process is started again it is difficult to achieve the same striking force straight away and this can result in a variation of the depth of the marks made.

There endless ways in which this technique can be utilized whether it is using readymade tools or making your own.

Rolling Mill

The rolling mill is designed to produce thinner gauges of sheet metal. Each mill has two horizontal highly polished hardened steel rollers, mounted so they sit parallel one above the other. There is a wheel on top of the mill to adjust the distance between the rollers to allow for the different thicknesses of metal, and an arm on the side of the mill to rotate the rollers manually.

The alternative use for the rolling mill is to create a texture on the surface of the metal. There is a restriction on the size of piece that can be textured caused by the width of the rollers; they vary in size from 8cm to 13cm width. Larger commercial ones are available but not so practical for a small workshop.

The objective is to create a pattern or texture on the pewter. There are several ways of achieving this but the main principle is that the metal and textured material is passed through the roller under pressure and the material will become embossed onto the surface of the pewter.

Creating a Pattern

Because the pewter is soft it can very easily pick up details. There are a number of ways to create a pattern:

Feathers, net, doilies, sandpaper and metal: Either cut out shapes or etched sheets of a harder material such as brass, wire, masking tape, string, material, textured paper, plastic or lace.

Rolling mill.

Sandpaper: If using a gritty material such as sandpaper make sure the rollers are cleaned thoroughly so they do not become damaged. It is a good idea to sandwich between card so none of the grit goes onto the rollers.

Etched sheet pattern: If you want to create multiples of the same pattern it is possible to etch the pattern onto a harder metal such as brass. This is then fed through the rollers and the pattern is embossed onto the pewter, with all the raised etched areas on the brass transferring to recessed areas in the pewter.

Cut-out metal pattern: Again using a harder material such as brass a pattern is cut out using a piercing saw, or circles can be made using various sizes of drilled holes. When this is put through the roller all the cut-out sections and drilled holes will

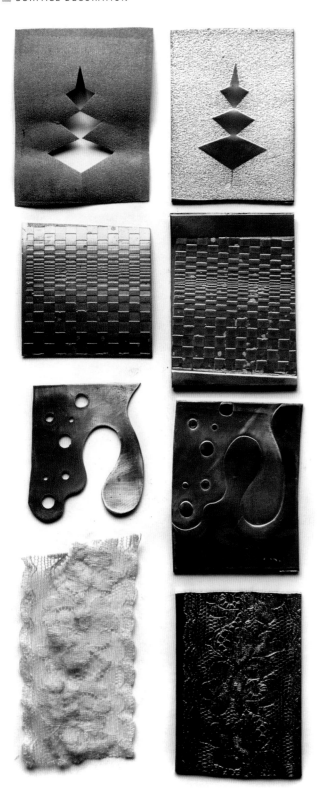

Commercial etched plates for rolling patterns (courtesy of A.R. Wentworth (Sheffield) Ltd).

appear as raised surfaces on the pewter, and areas where the metal touched will be recessed.

Soft materials: Materials such as fabric, paper or feathers are held in position while being fed through the rollers.

Commercial manufacturers use this technique as it produces larger quantities of patterned sheets quickly. Even a hammered texture can be etched onto a sheet; this is then fed through the roller and a hammered texture is instantly produced. As these templates are used considerably more than in a smaller workshop they need to be far more durable, so the designs are photo-etched onto magnesium sheets.

When using metal, especially steel, as a template it is advisable to create a sandwich around the patterned material or wire. This is not as important if using softer materials, but if using a steel sheet or wire this can damage rollers leaving permanent marks on them. These marks will then appear on every piece of metal that is put through the mill, and it can be an expensive process to get them removed. The piece being fed through the roller will be made of three layers: a back plate to your pattern, the pattern and the pewter sheet. If using an etched sheet, as long as it is not steel, just the two layers – the etched sheet and the pewter – can be fed through.

The same will apply if using the cut-out sheet. However if you want two symmetrical pieces, for example for a left and a right candlestick, positioning a sheet of pewter on the back and the front will give you two identical symmetrical patterned sheets.

Rolled pattern samples *top to bottom* sandpaper, etched brass plate, cut-out metal pattern and lace.

Feeding the metal and pewter into the rolling mill.

Rolling the Metal

Once the metal is prepared, put it in position ready to be fed into the rollers. It will be trial and error getting the correct distance between the rollers for creating an impression. Turn the wheel on top of the mill to adjust the rollers so they are a suitable distance apart, then feed through about 1cm to see if the pattern has been imprinted. If the rollers are too far apart there may be nothing at all. If it is too tight it could crush the material you are using, or if using a metal etched or cut-out template it could become stretched and distorted.

When you have checked the test piece and are happy that the pattern is correct, start to turn the arm and feed in the pewter. Once you start, roll the whole piece of metal through in one continuous movement; if stopped mid-way through it occasionally creates a line across the surface. The pattern should now be transferred onto the metal.

There are endless possibilities for using this technique and it is fruitful trying various materials to create different patterns. Keep a record of different samples with a written description so that you can refer back to it if needed at a future date.

It is worth noting that if the pattern is only lightly recessed into the metal, it may not be suitable for designs that are expected to withstand a lot of handling. As the pewter is soft, over a short period of time it may wear away. This could also

Rolled pewter and crystal necklace, Gill Clement (photographer Raffaella Sirtoli).

be a problem with regard to finishing a piece. If it needs to have a lot of work done to it while it is being constructed into a finished piece, care with processes such as emerying, filing and polishing will be needed.

Another consideration is that whatever pattern you are putting onto the pewter it will come out in reverse; remember this if using any letters or numbers within your design.

When you have finished using the rollers make sure they are cleaned, particularly if using gritty materials such as sandpaper for the pattern, as any small bits will then imprint onto metal put through the mill afterwards. It is also very important they are cleaned if in a shared workshop where precious metals are used, as there is a risk of contamination. Wiping down the rollers with a very fine wire wool will remove any bits and ensure that no pewter has been left on the rollers.

Colouring

Colouring is an area that has not been widely explored because pewter has such a low melting point. There are many processes that are used with other metals that rely on heat treatment, such as enamelling, using a blow torch and powder coating, which cannot be applied to pewter. It does not naturally change colour like copper, steel, titanium and brass when heat is applied. This does not mean however that there are no processes that can be used to create colour. There are techniques such as blackening, metal leafing, glass paints and cold enamel.

Blackening

Old antique pewter would naturally go grey over a period of time due to the lead content; however this is no longer the case and the pewter retains a polished finish. To replicate this grey finish solutions now have to be used. The piece can be completely blackened, or it can be brushed all over then areas removed; this creates contrast on a piece and can be used to highlight detail. It is particularly useful for *repoussé* work.

Before blackening an object the piece must be completed, including any polishing that needs to be done. There are several solutions available: Carr's Metal Black, usually used for blackening steel, and tourmaline, normally used for blacking brass. These do work, but they can leave a powdery residue on the surface. This can easily be removed with soapy water, but it can be a bit more difficult to remove on some complicated shapes. The tourmaline and Carr's solution are available in black or brown, the black giving a very dark grey finish and the brown a medium grey finish with a yellow tint.

It is also possible to make your own solution with 6 per cent nitric acid and 94 per cent distilled water. If mixing your own

solution it should be done with extreme caution, always wear rubber gloves, safety glasses and work in a ventilated area. Most important of all never add water to the acid, always add acid to the water.

When blackening a piece ensure that it is clean of oxide and grease, as both of these will hinder the blackening process and the solution may not work at all or create a very patchy finish. If it has an oxidized finish it may need another polish. Once a piece has been polished the surface should be wiped with a methylated spirit to remove any grease that will act as a barrier against the solution. Once it is completely clean wipe the solution over the surface using a brush or cotton wool; if there are lots of details it may be better to use a brush to get into all the areas. It should visibly start to go black quite quickly. Once the piece is completely black rinse it to remove the excess solution and dry it thoroughly with a soft cloth.

If you want to create a contrast with polished and blackened areas when working on a small piece or a *repoussé* design, where detail could easily be lost on a polishing mop, use Brasso and a soft duster to rub over the surface removing the black surface from all of the highpoints. If it is a larger piece it will be easier to work on the bench polisher, using a soft mop and rouge. With both methods the pieces will need to be cleaned with hot soapy water to remove compound left by the polisher and any Brasso residue.

Cupra: Copper Colour Finish

Cupra is another cold patinating solution similar to tourmaline. It is normally used to make metals such as bronze and brass go green, but when used on pewter it produces a copper colour. It is vital again that the surface is completely clean, no grease or even fingerprints, particularly with this solution as it can cause problems getting an even finish.

Left to right cupra, gold leaf, pumice, polished, blackened then polished, and blackened.

Before applying the solution the surface must be completely free of grease; you can either use methylated or a kitchen scourer with hot water and a detergent. When the piece is clean, use a soft cloth or cotton wool to apply the cupra all over the surface. Wear rubber gloves while applying the solution to avoid skin contact. The colour will start to appear quite quickly; however for a more intense colour the pewter will probably need several layers. It also helps with the colouring if the old solution is rinsed off with hot soapy water before a new layer is applied. Once the desired colour has been achieved and the piece has been rinsed and dried thoroughly, buff the surface by rubbing the piece quite vigorously with a soft silver polishing cloth, which will make the copper surface finish become more reflective. It can then be sealed with Ormoline sealer to protect this finish.

Metal Leafing/Gilding

Metal leafing is a simple and more economic way of applying a different metal colour to the surface to create a decorative and contrasting finish. The metal leaf sheets come in books, with each sheet of metal backed with a tissue. They come in a wide variety of colours; it is also possible to buy pure gold and silver leaf, but these are more expensive.

Pure gold leaf and fine silver leaf will not tarnish whereas the other imitation metals will, so once completed they will need to be varnished to avoid this. Imitation gold leaf comes in a variety of names, such as Dutch metal, brass leaf and composition leaf. Aluminium leaf is used for imitation silver, and you can get copper leaf. There is also variegated leaf, which comes in sheets which produce random patterns in different brightly colours of red, blue or green.

Unlike plating, the gilding/leafing is not as durable; this should be considered if using it on a piece that may be in constant use. It is possible to build up layers of the leaf to make it thicker, but over time it will rub away if there is heavy usage, so it is really only advisable to be used for decorative purposes.

EQUIPMENT
- Fine wire wool or emery paper (600 grade)
- Brush
- Size (fast drying size takes 30–60 minutes; slow drying size, more suitable for large areas, takes 12–16 hours)
- Masking tape, if areas are needed to be masked off
- Metal leaf sheet
- Sharp scissors or scalpel
- Varnish

Before setting up your work area ensure there are no drafts from open doors and windows, as this can blow the sheets of leaf around and make it difficult to work.

To prepare the metal for gilding it should be completely free of grease and the surface rubbed with a fine wire wool; this helps the size adhere to the metal. If you are applying the metal only to certain areas you can mask them off with masking tape to stop the areas not being gilded from being scratched.

Use the brush to apply an even layer of the size over the sections to be gilded; being careful not to go beyond the desired boundaries; again areas can be masked off with tape if needed.

Leave the size to dry. It is ready for the leaf when it has become tacky, this can vary depending upon the room temperature and the thickness of the layer of size applied. Rather than using your finger, which will leave grease on the surface, use your knuckle to test the size; you should feel some resistance when pulling your knuckle away.

Cut a piece of the metal foil. It does not need to fit the area exactly; if it is slightly larger it is better as it allows some flexibility when positioning it onto the pewter. Using the brush lift the metal foil and place it gently onto the pewter and size; if the area is not completely covered cut another piece and add it, making sure you overlap the previous piece.

As the size is tacky the foil will stick to the surface. Gently rub the surface with a soft cloth, if the base shape is irregular a brush can be used to rub it into any difficult areas. Rubbing over the surface will remove any excess foil and will also reveal any areas that mistakenly did not have any size, so revealing the pewter; these can be rectified by brushing on more of the size and repeating the process.

Pumice: Matt Finish

To give the surface of the pewter a matt finish, as well as using the scotch mops (described in Chapter 6) it is also possible to use pumice powder. Pumice is frozen volcanic glass; it is known as glass because it has no crystal structure. It is very porous, lightweight, white/grey in colour and can float in water. It is ground into a fine dust and used as an abrasive; it

Pumicing the pewter.

Cards, Caroline Fielding.

comes in various grades that can be added to water or oil, so it can be mixed into a paste to be used.

When used for more commercial polishing pumice is mixed with oil and placed in a tray under the polishing motor. As the mops rotate the pumice is thrown onto the mops and removes any surface defects. This is a very messy process and mainly used when polishing on a large scale.

On a smaller scale pumice can be used to create a matt finish on the surface of the pewter. A small amount of pumice is mixed with water and made into a paste, which is rubbed onto the surface using a toothbrush. This produces an even matt finish.

It is important that the piece is polished before using the pumice, as the pumice is a very fine finish and any scratches will show through. If you want a combination of matt and polished finish, once the piece has been polished areas can be masked off with masking tape and then pumiced.

When complete, remove the tape and rinse thoroughly to remove any excess pumice, so that when dried with a soft cloth there is none left to create scratches in the polished areas.

Glass Paint

Glass paint is ideal for using on pewter as it is designed to stick to a non-absorbent surface. It works most successfully on items with low relief designs and textures. As it is only a paint it will not fill areas like cold enamel. The paint is normally used on stained glass, so the lead acts as a barrier stopping the paint leaking. To control this when used with pewter, use on areas that are slightly raised around the edge to keep it contained.

The paint comes in a variety of rich colours. They are translucent so you will see the metal through it, unlike the opaque cold enamel. This can create interesting effects if painted over a textured surface, as it is similar to that of the jewellery technique, champlevé, where the metal is etched or engraved, then covered with a translucent vitreous enamel.

Before using the paint the pewter must be clean. To degrease simply use soapy water or alcohol. The paint is then brushed carefully into the desired areas.

Glass paint is an ideal medium for low relief *repoussé* work, such as work by **Caroline Fielding**. Caroline produces a range of cards and notebooks with low relief pewter *repoussé* details on the front and uses the paint like an enamel to add colour and contrast to her designs.

There are a variety of paints available, some that are air dried and some that specify to be put in an oven to harden, to enable the glass to be put in a dishwasher. Since the pewter cannot be put in a dishwasher you are not limited to specific types.

Plating

There are numerous types of plating – gold, copper, silver, rhodium, nickel and chrome. They are used for a variety of reasons: for creating a decorative finish, a harder wearing surface, or in some cases such as gold plating it can also be used in electrics and engineering.

There are two methods of plating: one is electroplating, where electricity is passed through an acidic solution containing the metal, for example gold. The other is chemical plating, where a catalytic reaction takes the place of the electricity. It is possible to plate pewter, although it is not the easiest. The most common plating, used mainly for decorative reasons, is gold.

In order to gold plate pewter, however, it first needs to be copper plated, then nickel plated, prior to the gold. The gold will not bond with the pewter directly, so the copper plate is applied first. However if the gold plate is applied direct to the copper it has a dull appearance. To compensate for this, a nickel plate is applied to the copper, and then the gold plate on top of the nickel; this then gives the gold a bright shiny appearance.

Areas can also be masked off. This piece was etched with the design, then the raised areas were painted with nail varnish to act as a resist to the plating.

Etched then gold-plated sample.

Cold Enamel

Cold enamel is used predominantly in the large scale production of fashion jewellery. It is an economical and quick way to colour a piece, and ideal for using on metal, which is why it is used on a lot of high street jewellery. Unlike vitreous enamelling, which uses a glass powder that has to be heated in a kiln for the glass to fuse together, cold enamel is mixed with a hardener, then left to cool at air temperature. Because of the low melting point of the pewter vitreous enamelling is not an option, as the whole piece would melt if put in a kiln at the temperature required to melt the glass.

There are various types of cold enamel. The most commonly available from craft suppliers comes in two parts – a coloured enamel and a hardener – which work on a ratio of two parts colour to one part hardener. Other types are available and ratio does vary; for example some come as a clear enamel and a coloured powder is added. Whichever type is used it is important to follow the guidelines for mixing.

These were made with the coloured enamel with the hardener added to it.

EQUIPMENT
- Coloured enamel
- Hardener
- Newspaper
- Mixing Cups
- Stirring sticks/Cocktail sticks depending on quantities being mixed
- Syringe (optional)
- White spirit
- Gloves and apron

When using the cold enamel if you want to create deep sections of the enamel it is important that there is a bezel (a raised piece of metal) to hold it. If the bezel has been soldered check that the solder has flowed all the way round as the liquid enamel will leak through even the smallest pin hole.

If using more than one colour, draw a plan to use as a reference while doing the colouring, to limit the risk of putting the colours in the wrong place. Select the colours to be used, along with a measuring cup and stirring stick for each colour. An ideal working temperature for the enamel is 20°C; an increase in the temperature can result in the enamel solidifying more quickly.

Make sure you are not working in a dusty environment,

Cold enamel samples: enamel poured onto the surface of the walnut; enamel poured into contained areas.

as any dust that falls onto the surface of the piece is impossible to remove. Lay newspaper on the work surface as it can become quite messy. It is also an idea to wear rubber gloves and an apron to protect hands and clothing.

Pour the enamel into the measuring cup using enough to fill the hollow. Then add the hardener ensuring you are using the correct quantities (two parts colour to one part hardener). If there is not enough hardener it can result in the enamel not setting, and too much can cause it to set too quickly. Thoroughly mix the two together with the stirring stick/cocktail stick. Then leave to stand for 10 minutes. This allows any air bubbles to be released. Gently tapping the pot on the worktop will also help any air bubbles to float to the surface.

Once the enamel has settled it can be poured onto the piece. It can be poured directly from the pot, or you can use the stick to feed it in; the cocktail stick is useful as the point allows you to put the enamel in more difficult spaces. If you are enamelling quite intricate areas a syringe can also be used.

If the enamel spills where it is not needed white spirit can be used to remove it; a small piece of tissue wrapped around a cocktail stick and dipped in white spirit or a cotton bud can

help to clean small areas. Once the enamel is set it is very difficult to remove. Thin areas can be removed with emery although the metal will then need to be re-polished, but for larger deeper areas it is not really possible.

The enamel is workable for about an hour depending on room temperature, but will then start to thicken considerably. It should be left for 24 hours to cure completely. Do not be tempted to touch the surface beforehand as it will leave fingerprints on the surface. If you do want to be able to test it put a small amount on a scrap piece of pewter and test this.

Colours can be mixed beforehand in the mixing pot or different colours can be added later. Once poured this can also create different effects as a darker colour disperses into a lighter one, or colours can be manipulated with a cocktail stick or piece of wire creating lines of colour. If using the enamel for the first time try making a few samples to explore the various effects.

The natural finish of the enamel is gloss, but you can create a matt finish with the steam from a kettle. Before the enamel is completely hard, 3–4 hours after being poured, if you hold the piece over the kettle the steam vapour will make the surface go matt, and the enamel will then keep this finish. If using steam, wipe away any condensation that has formed on the pewter with a soft cloth, or it will dry and create watermarks on the polished surface.

Clean any brushes and syringes with white spirit before the enamel has dried. All enamelling work should be done when the piece is complete as if any further hammering or soldering work is done on the piece it will damage the enamel. In this piece the enamel was poured quite thickly into certain areas. For the walnut casting the enamel was brushed on and then due to the shape the enamel slowly moved into the grooves, highlighting the recesses with the red colour.

Eureka Bowl designed by Nina Tolstrup, produced by A. R. Wentworth (Sheffield) Ltd.

EXPERIMENTAL COLOURING TECHNIQUES

Helgi Joensen is influenced by the ocean, the Midnight Sun, the Northern Lights and the rugged coastline of Norway. This wall piece is made in slate and pewter, and the colour is created through a process of oxidization. Each piece is constructed and the texture is created by partially melting the surface of the pewter.

Soap Dispenser, GNZ Designs.

Trish Woods is a jeweller and tutor at South Devon College. As part of her PhD work exploring potential processes for colouration of pewter and their creative applications, she has developed a chemical process which aims to utilize the colours inherent but hidden in tin and pewter.

Ring, designed to cut across the hand and contrast with its form, with a flash of colour as the hand moves, Trish Woods (photographer Dominic Brandi).

Bangles, Trish Woods.

Tom Neal is a pewtersmith who explores and adapts colouring techniques for pewter using an anodizing technique, to produce subtle colour changes on the surface of the pewter.

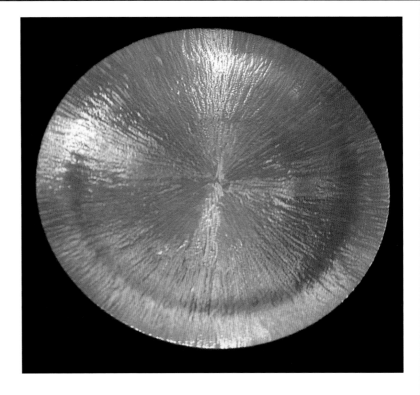

Plate, Tom Neal (courtesy of The Worshipful Company of Pewterers).

Roma Vincent developed an unconventional heating process which alters the crystalline structure of the pewter elements of tin, copper and antimony. The gradual and repetitive heating process coaxes an array of vibrant colours to the surface of the pewter. The pewter is also fused and forged with silver and other semi-precious metals to create contrasts of different layers and textures.

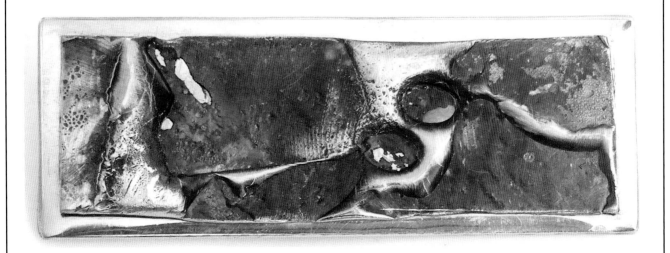

Grike Brooch, Roma Vincent.

Selection of mallets used on pewter.

CHAPTER 5

SHAPING AND FORMING PEWTER

Fabricating Pewter

Many of the techniques for using pewter are similar to those for working with other metals – it can be raised, spun, folded, hollowed, or chased. The processes do however need to be adapted to allow for the different properties of the pewter.

One of the main differences when shaping pewter is that it does not need to be annealed. In this technique, which is used on other metals such as silver, copper and brass, the metal is heated to a specific temperature or colour and then allowed to cool slowly to soften it prior to it being used so the material can be shaped more easily. Annealing is carried out intermittently on other metals, because repetitive hammering and working work hardens the metal, reduces its ductility (making it more breakable) and can increase brittleness. Pewter however is not affected in the same way, so the annealing process is not necessary. If stamping a form and using a thick gauge of pewter sheet immersing the pewter in boiling water can soften it slightly to help the pewter press into the former.

HAMMERS AND MALLETS

Some metal hammers may be used when working with pewter, particularly if texturing or planishing (smoothing out curves on dished or raised metal). However it is better to use mainly wooden, rawhide, nylon or rubber mallets. As the pewter is soft these will leave less marks on the surface so lessen the amount of cleaning up when a piece has been completed. Make sure when using all wooden or rawhide mallets and tools that no metal becomes embedded in the head, as if it is then used to hammer work it will leave deep marks in the pewter.

Rawhide mallet: Available in a variety of sizes and weights, this is useful for general pewter working whether it is shaping it round a stake or flattening a sheet.

Bossing mallet: These egg-shaped mallets are made from a high density wood such as lignum vitae or boxwood. The different sizes and lengths means that they can have a variety of uses whether for a high sided bowl or a large shallow flat dish.

Nylon mallet: General use mallet.

Rubber mallet: These are ideal for large areas where it is important to keep it smooth.

Lead-working tools: These come in a wide variety of shapes and sizes and can sometimes be just what is needed for a specific job.

Paper mallet: A traditional mallet made to be used on pewter is a paper mallet. This is ideal for pewter as it does not mark the metal and can be made very simply. A piece of paper is rolled very tightly to a slightly wider width than you want the mallet to be. When it has been rolled wrap it in sticky brown gum paper to hold it all in place. When dry cut it to length, with a band saw if you have access to one, or if not a wood saw will work too. Wrap string around either end of the paper roll several times; this will stop the roll bursting open when it is used to strike the pewter. The head can then be drilled and a handle fed through the hole and secured.

Stakes and formers: These are shapes used for shaping metal over, on and into, with hammers and mallets. Wooden or steel formers and stakes are preferable. Due to the softness of the pewter it is possible to use a wooden former for a number of years without it being badly damaged. This also means that stakes and formers can be produced quite cheaply either by a wood turner, or even some everyday household objects can be adapted. As long as they are made of a hard wood so they will not easily split when pewter is being hammered onto it, if making your own consideration should also be given to how the stake will be held in a vice so that it can be safely hammered onto.

Sand bag: This is a heavy-duty leather circular bag filled with sand. The pewter is placed on top of the bag and then struck with a mallet; the sand gives support, but also yields enough so a flat sheet can be shaped into items such as bowl. Care should be taken to avoid sharp objects that may pierce the leather resulting in sand leaking.

Hollowed wooden blocks: This is a technique is traditional for all types of metalworkers to produce a bowl, either using a hollowed out wooden block or a tree trunk (which is good for noise reduction and stability). It is better to have a variety of sizes of blocks, so the size of your bowl is not limited to two or three sizes, starting with a shallow shape for a free standing bowl, working through to a deeper more curved base that will produce a rounded bowl which will not be free standing and will need some sort of support to keep it upright.

Mallet made and used for thirty years by pewterer Tom Neal.

Examples of various wooden stakes and formers.

EXERCISE
Sugar Bowl

EQUIPMENT

- ▨ Pewter sheet 1.5mm
- ▨ Large wooden mallet
- ▨ Sage file
- ▨ Flat file
- ▨ Scriber (a fine-pointed piece of steel used like a pencil)
- ▨ Piercing saw and Blades (size 0)
- ▨ Emery paper 220
- ▨ Emery stick (400 paper)
- ▨ Dividers
- ▨ Doming block and punches
- ▨ Blocking hammer (for texturing different size heads will vary the texture)
- ▨ Soldering equipment
- ▨ Polishing equipment
- ▨ Wooden forming bowls
- ▨ 2mm drill

Hammering the pewter into the wooden former.

Set the dividers to a 5cm width; this will produce a 10cm diameter circle. Mark the circle on the sheet; then using the piercing saw cut out the shape. Using the flat file, file all around the edge of the circle removing any high points and the marks left by the saw. Then using the emery stick emery around the edge to remove the file marks, and when completed remove any sharp burrs on the upper and lower side of the metal, as these could damage the former.

Using a forming bowl that is slightly larger than the disc, position your disc in the former. There will be a mark made by the dividers when initially marking the circle; position the side with the mark in the bowl so the centre point is directly against the wood.

Start to gently raise the outside edge by hammering the perimeter with the blocking mallet, overlapping each hammer mark as you move around the edge of the bowl. You do not want to be too heavy with the mallet initially, as this will cause folds and dents that will be hard to remove. It is important that any burrs have been removed from the disc as these will cut into the former and will create marks that will transfer onto the metal.

When starting to hammer make sure you are holding the handle towards the end away from the head with a firm grip, as holding it too near to the head creates an imbalance and it is difficult to strike the metal with any force. Holding it towards the end, with your index finger

extended along the hammer, enables each strike to be done with control.

Always ensure you are supporting the edge on the wooden bowl. You want to achieve a smooth edge to the bowl with no dents and folds. Once the outer edge has been done you can start to increase the pressure of the mallet; this can be done by raising the height of the mallet and increasing the force. Once you become used to using the mallet and the former you will start to develop a rhythm striking the metal and slowly turning the bowl.

Keep the strokes overlapping each other so dents do not occur, slowly working round and down into the former to create the bowl. When the bowl sits comfortably in the former, transfer it into the smaller former.

Hold the bowl in the former at a slight angle; as it is unlikely to fit in straight away you will need to bring in the perimeter. Support the edge of the bowl on the former with the opposite side raised so it is not touching the wood. (If it is touching as you start to hammer it will hit the edge of the wood and create dents that will be difficult to remove.) Repeat the process of overlapping the hammering, moving around and down into the bowl until it sits neatly in the smaller former.

At intermittent stages remove the bowl from the former and use sight and touch to see if there are any raised bumps or irregularities; this can be done by running your hand over the surface or lifting the bowl and slowly rotating it looking at the profile. If there are irregularities place it back in the former and work on these areas.

It also possible to use other formers, for example a round ball shape that is the appropriate size, to work from the outside of the bowl. You will need to create your initial bowl shape, but then instead of working from the inside, sit the pewter bowl over the round ball former and repeat the overlapping gentle hammering but this time from the centre to the outside edge. You may prefer to alternate between the two processes working from the inside then out.

If working from the outside of the bowl, your position in relation to the piece as you are hammering is important, not only in being able to execute the right pressure but ensuring you do not put strain on your shoulders and back. The stake you will be working on should be level with your forearm when your arm is in the horizontal position after completing a strike to the stake. If it is too high

Shaping the bowl from the outside.

prolonged hammering can cause your arm, shoulders and back to be hunched and this can create problems. Sometimes it may be necessary to have a step to stand on that will bring you to the correct height.

Once the bowl is completed place it back in the former to support it while making the textured finish. Consider whether you would like the hammered finish to be all over the bowl or just on a small section of it. Once you have decided select a hammer; if you want small dimples use the smaller head or similarly if you want larger marks use the larger hammer.

Before starting to hammer check the surface of the hammer. It should have a polished finish; if there are any scratches or marks on it these will transfer onto your bowl. It may be they are very light marks and can be removed on the polishing mop, but if they are heavier it may need to be emeryed with a fine paper then polished. If you do emery the surface be careful not to alter the shape of the head.

When hammering ensure the bowl is constantly supported by the wood; if it is not it will alter the profile. If it does distort use the mallet again and gently tap it back into place. Once the texturing is finished you will need to make the base so the bowl will be stable. Set the dividers to 1.5cm using the centre mark created at the beginning when marking out the disc, and mark out a circle (diameter 3cm). Drill a hole on the inside of the circle ensuring you keep within the line, then using your piercing saw cut out the hole.

To cut the hole you will need to undo one end of the saw; it is easier to do the end furthest away, and then push the blade through the hole with the marked out circle facing away from you as you need to see the line while cutting. The bowl will need to be supported while setting up the frame as if left the weight will break the blade. Once you have the correct tension in the blade tighten the nut and start to pierce out the circle. If you do not feel confident enough to pierce directly on the line cut slightly on the inside as any excess can be filed away.

It will feel awkward initially as it is not a flat shape that is being cut and this may cause more blades to snag and break. Work at your own pace slowly rotating the bowl as you cut out the hole. Once the whole circle has been cut, you will need to loosen the nut holding the blade, again supporting the weight of the bowl with your other hand as you do it. When the blade has been removed use an oval file to neaten up the cut-out circle.

Set the dividers to 1.6mm and on a separate piece of pewter mark out another circle. Cut this out, again using

Doming the disc to fit into the cut-out hole at the base of the texture bowl.

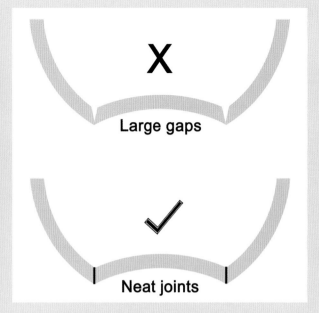

Fitting the dome ready for soldering.

the piercing saw; then file around the edge. File off any sharp burrs. Then select a suitable punch and dome for your disc taking into account the thickness of the metal; it must not be too little as the edge of the metal will fold and distort. Place the disc of pewter in the doming block. Using a ball pein hammer strike the punch so the pewter is forced into the dome. Move the punch around the edges and down into the middle so the pewter eventually is in direct contact with the steel all the way round.

Once the dome sits into the steel block comfortably, reduce the size of the punch and hole. You do not need to make it too domed; a shallow curve is all that is needed – it is solely to produce a stable base for the bowl. Check regularly that it is still fitting neatly in the hole cut out in the bottom of the bowl. When the dome is complete place a piece of 400 emery paper on a flat plate and rub the dome over the surface until the top is completely flat. Once it is

flat start to file the outside perimeter of the dome until it fits neatly into the base of the bowl. It should sit with the concave part to the outside so there is a flat base to the bowl.

When the dome sits neatly in the bowl, it can then be soldered in place. Set up the bowl in the soldering area so it is in an upright position with the dome in place. Both joints will be clean, as they have just been filed. Brush flux all around the joint. Then position several paillions of solder around the joint. Gently heat both pieces evenly and solder the two pieces together; be prepared with extra solder just in case it is needed. Once it has completely cooled wash with warm soapy water and dry.

The base needs to be made completely flat. Again using the flat plate, this time with a coarser paper 220 grit, to start with slowly move the bowl backwards and forwards until it is completely flat and looks like just one piece of metal, not two joined together. When the bottom is flat, turn the bowl upside down and repeat until the rim of the bowl also sits flat on the steel plate. The process will also need to be repeated on both top and bottom with a fine 400 emery paper.

To make the rim measure the diameter of the shaped pewter bowl. Then using a compass mark a circle the relevant size on a piece of paper; this can then be used as the basis for the template. Draw several designs on paper, cut

Soldering the dome into the bowl to create a stable flat base.

them out and try each on the bowl looking to see which one will work best. If you do not have a deep throat saw be careful not to make the design so big that it cannot be cut with a standard size saw frame. As it is likely that the bowl will be used with the spoon made during the cuttlefish exercise you may want to link it with some of the design elements used for that so they become a set.

On a separate sheet of pewter using a pair of dividers mark a circle the same diameter as the bowl. Then match the line on the pewter with the line on the circle of the paper template and scribe around the decorative template outer edge. Start to cut out the outside of the shape using a piercing saw; you may find the rim too wide to use with the normal size jeweller's saw and will need to use a deep throat saw instead. These take a bit of practice to control as the frame is so much deeper, but the depth enables the whole shape to be cut in one without the need to keep taking the blade out and start at a different angle. It may be that the design is quite narrow so this will be unnecessary, but it is something to consider.

Once the whole shape has been cut out it is easier to file and emery the outside edge before the inside circle is cut to fit onto the bowl, as this could make it quite narrow in places and it may bend and become misshapen as it is filed. When the edge is completed drill a hole on the inside of the scribed circle, as done with the smaller dome, and cut out the central circle again keeping on the inside of the line. If the hole becomes too big it will mean remaking the whole rim as the gap between the bowl and the rim will be too large to solder.

When the rim is complete begin to fit the bowl to the lid. There will probably be some adjustments needed with the file; try to take very little off at a time and keep checking it regularly. Place the rim on a completely flat surface to make sure it is flat; if it is not it will be easy to push flat with your hands or use a rawhide mallet. Turn the bowl upside down and push it into the hole; you want to have a close fit before soldering it together.

Now that both joints are in place transfer the bowl in the same position to the soldering area, brush flux around the whole joint and start to heat both pieces equally. It is possible to place small pallions on the joint as before, but as it is a larger area you may find it easier to stick solder the pieces together (*see* Chapter 2).

Once soldered and the piece has cooled wash in warm soapy water to remove the flux and then dry with a soft cloth. When the bowl is placed the right way up you should be able to see a neat joint; this edge now needs to be filed to make it look like one piece of metal. Use an oval or half-round file to work around the inside rim of the bowl filing a curved edge; this will make the rim look like it flows into the bowl. If the file has a pointed end be careful not to push the file too far across and scratch the inside of the opposite wall.

This filed edge now needs to be emeryed ready for polishing. The emery stick will probably be too large. Cut off a small square of emery paper and tightly fold it around a flat needle file. This can then be used to work slowly around the rim removing all the file marks.

The bowl is now complete and ready for polishing. These bowls were made with different finishes: one was polished; the other was blackened, then some of the patinated finish was removed with a Scotch-Brite mop to produce a contrasting finish.

Soldering on the rim.

The finished bowls: one highly polished and the other blackened then pumiced to create a contrasting matt finish.

Pewter Sheet Fabrication

When working with pewter sheet it is important to consider what the final piece will be used for and how it will be constructed, as pewter is quite soft in comparison to other metals. This softness and flexibility does however mean it lends itself to many processes, and the way the object is made can give the design strength.

Many techniques used are the same as silversmithing/metalworking techniques. The sheet can be hand-formed, scored, manipulated around formers, and then soldered together.

A lot of designer/makers fabricate their designs from sheet. The Dessert Plate and Cream Jug were made by **Jennifer Kidd**, which was inspired by the carnivorous pitcher plant and Venus fly trap. This design was made from sheet pewter that was hand formed and soldered together.

American designer/craftsmen **Jon Michael Route** combines metalsmithing, craft and art to produce beautifully crafted sculptural designs. His teapots play with the notion of function, and his collection of teapot sculptures plays with the idea of the teapot. To Jon, the teapot embodies most of what he thinks of as metalsmithing as seen in his Teapot with Wild Hair made in 2006.

Desert plate and cream jug, Jennifer Kidd.

Tea Pot with Wild Hair, Jon Michael Route (photographer Deb Route).

EXERCISE

Fabricated Vase

EQUIPMENT

- Thin card
- Template
- Scriber
- Metal ruler
- Pewter sheet
- Scoring tool (These can be bought but can also be easily made using a piece of mild steel, by cutting one end to a tapered point, and filing the edge at an angle so it will cut into the metal; as the angles that will be created in the vase are not made to specific dimensions it is not necessary to be exact.)
- Dividers
- Jeweller's saw
- Pillar drill and drill bit
- Emery stick
- Flat file
- Pumice powder
- Soldering equipment
- Tin snips

Use the template at the back of the book for a constructed vase. Trace the outline and the two internal circles, and stick the design to a thin piece of card. Using a scriber draw round the design to transfer it onto the pewter. Make a mark to show the top and bottom of each line that will be folded, then using a scriber and steel ruler join the two marks together. You may want to use dividers for the two circles to ensure they are accurate and just use the pencil lines as a guide to where they should be placed.

Cut around the outside edge of the line with a piercing saw. Once this is complete drill a small hole on the inside of the line of both circles; this is then used to put the saw blade through to cut the holes. Pierce out the holes. Use the file, then emery stick, all around the edge of the sheet and the inside of the circles removing any burrs.

Place the pewter on a piece of wood, to prevent the scouring tool slipping and cutting into the worktop; or you may prefer to put it on a piece of rubber matting to hold it in place. Using a scriber and a steel ruler scribe deeply over the three lines running vertically on the design; these help the scoring tool to locate while making the grooves for folding. If the scored lines are not very deep it is easy to slip and create deep scratches across the surface, which will then be very difficult to remove.

Using the scoring tool and ruler start slightly in from the outside edge of the pewter (because it is difficult to draw the scoring tool in from the edge of the metal). Asserting pressure draw the tool down the line created with the scriber; repeat this several times, then turn the sheet upside down and repeat so the groove is cut across the whole piece.

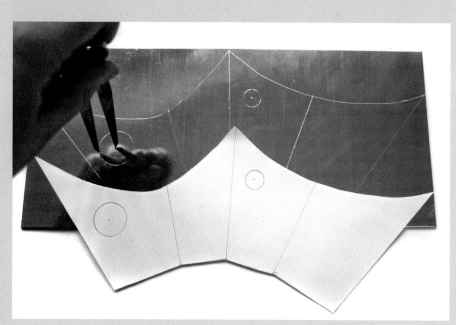

Marking the outline on the pewter sheet.

Scoring the lines for folding the shape.

Repeat this process on all three lines until each is approximately three quarters of the way into the pewter. Once complete, draw a line 3mm in from the two side edges of the pewter from top to bottom. Using a coarse file, file this section away to a tapered point; when the two ends meet after it has been folded it will create a neat sharp joint to fit in with the other corners.

Start to fold up the vase on each scored line. You may wish to place a piece of wood across the scored line to fold the pewter up against it so the sides remain flat and

Soldering the vase together.

do not curve. The two ends should meet to make a sharp corner joint. Binding wire is then wrapped around the whole piece to hold it in place while you then solder the two ends together. Then wash with warm soapy water to remove the flux. The inside is going to be made matt so using a toothbrush and pumice powder mixed with water into a paste, brush the inside of the vase with the paste until all the interior has an even matt finish.

For the base, a piece of the excess that was cut from the initial rectangle of pewter should be large enough; this can also be pumiced on one side before soldering. Thoroughly rinse off all the pumice powder, then solder the main body onto the base (the matt surface of the base facing upwards into the vase), using a stick of

solder and turntable so the piece can be rotated while soldering.

Once the base has been soldered on, use a pair of snips to cut off the excess pewter. It is preferable and easier to use the snips instead of a saw, as the nuts on the end of the saw can sometimes scrape against the surface of the vase making deep scratches. When all the excess has been removed all the soldered edges can then be cleaned up with a file and then emery paper covered in a 400 grit.

The vase is then ready to be polished. Move the vase in one direction, being careful the mop does not catch on the holes. Once it has been polished is should be washed in soapy water to remove the polishing compound. The pumice may need to be redone in certain areas. The outside particularly around the holes and top edge can be covered with masking tape; this will stop the pumice from marking the polished surface. The vase is then complete.

Using snips to remove the excess sheet on the base.

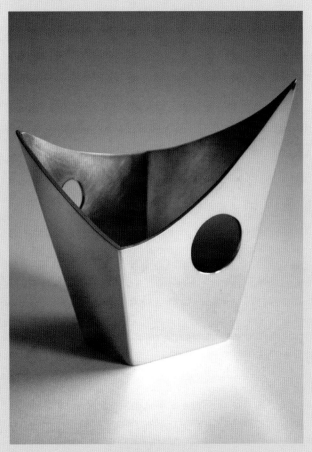

Completed vase.

Torsion Vases (pair), Toby Russell
(photographer Jeoff Howes).

Designer/silversmith **Toby Russell** uses his silversmithing techniques for several pieces that he has designed in pewter. The Torsion Vase/s was made from one sheet of pewter, which was scored, folded and soldered. He incorporates a feeling of movement around his designs by way of interlocking facets, the highly reflective quality of the pewter integral in distorting the environment around the piece by means of form alone without the need for detail of ornamentation.

understanding of the process, its capabilities and limitations will enable you to design work relevant for the process.

EQUIPMENT
Lathe: The lathe is used to rotate the former as metal is being spun over it; it should be heavy duty enough to withstand the heavy pressure that is needed to manipulate the metal, particularly if working on larger pieces.

Spinning

The basic principle of spinning is forcing a circular disc of metal over a former until the metal fits tightly and reproduces the shape of the former. Spinning was first introduced into England in the fourteenth century. It was such a skilled vocation that a guild was established to control the quality of the craftsmanship.

Spinning is a very traditional working technique for pewter; the softness of the metal lends itself to the process. It is a specialized technique that is very skilled and not many people can do it today. It is unlikely that it is a technique for a small workshop, as it is improbable that the quantities of products being produced in this way will warrant the set-up costs and time that would need to be spent learning the process.

It is however useful to have an understanding of the process as there may be times when a design could use the technique, and you may need a spinner to make something for you. An

Spinning lathe set-up with chuck and tools.

Chuck/formers: The formers can be made from several materials: steel, brass, nylon and wood. If using wood it should be a hard wood, as a soft wood will not give a smooth, even finish and if the metal was spun over a soft wood it would pick up these details and the inside would be marked. If made of metal it should also be polished to avoid the possibility of marking the inside.

Positioning the disc ready to be spun.

Drawing the metal over the former.

Spinning the bowl on air.

Split nylon former.

The former should be tapered so when the article is spun it will lift straight off. It is however possible to make more complex shapes by producing formers that will break down into sections or split in the middle. This allows for concave designs to be part of the design.

A skilled spinner will also be able to do what is known as spinning on air. This process was used in the bowl designed by **Miranda Watkins** that is produced by Wentworth. This is a challenging bowl to make for the most experienced of spinners due to the size, thickness of the metal and complex profile.

Forming tools: There are many shapes of tools available, each being suited to a particular job whether it is burnishing, trimming, drawing down and forming or beading. They are large in size being about 60cm long, half of that being the handle. This is due to the handle needing to be held under the arm to get the leverage to move the metal. The forged, shaped ends are polished and rounded so they will not mark the surface of the metal, apart from the trimming tool, which is made sharp in order to cut the pewter.

If the form is quite shallow it may be spun on one former, but if it has more depth it may require a series of formers before reaching the desired height. The metal is clamped between the former and what is known as the follow block. The tool rest is adjusted so it does not come in contact with the metal and is just below the centre line; the peg is put just to the right of the disc when spinning. The tool is then positioned between the peg and the disc for working the metal.

Finished Groove Bowl, designed by Miranda Watkins, produced by A.R Wentworth (Sheffield) Ltd (photographer Graham Pym).

Prior to spinning a grease or wax is applied to the surface to enable the tools to move smoothly across the surface. A back stick is positioned on the other side of the disc to support the metal. Both the spinning tool and back stick work in unison as the metal is moved over the former, the spinning tool using the peg as leverage, and as the metal moves over the former the peg is moved along the tool rest to maintain the leverage and support.

An experienced spinner can produce items very quickly, and it is fascinating to watch as the metal slowly envelops the former, to become a seamless raised form.

Paper Cups and Plates: stamped plates and spun cups, Tim Parsons.

movement increases the force, considerably forcing the tool or punch into the metal placed centrally underneath.

Many heavy metal workers and blacksmiths use the fly-press to punch out holes in sheet metal, rather than cutting or drilling. Punch and dies are also used to stamp out shapes. A punch can be made with a die that it closely fits into; the punch is inserted into the central column and the die is placed below with the metal sheet placed over the top. The pressure then forces the metal into the die producing either a flat punched-out shape or a more three-dimensional stamped-out shape.

Fly-press.

Fly-Pressing/Stamping

The fly-press is a useful tool to stamp out multiples of a shape quickly and easily without a lot of expensive tooling. It was invented in about 1500 initially for stamping out coins and then went on to also be used for pressing, punching and forging.

It works with manual force rather than electricity, by using heavy counterweights. The overhead handle, which is counterbalanced with a heavy steel ball/fly weight, is turned up and down a large central thread, with a steel block for holding tools positioned at the bottom. The handle is turned up the central thread, then released. The weight on the arm helps to maintain the momentum as the arm twists around the central thread, and because of the weight this small downward

Because more precision equipment and processes, such as laser cutting, have now been developed many fly-presses have become redundant, so it is quite easy to find a second-hand one relatively cheaply.

They come in various sizes starting from 45–50cm frame height up to 112–125cm. The most common sizes are the 0, 1 and 2, starting with 0 (45–50cm), 1 (47.5–52.5cm) and 2 (50–60cm). The smallest 0 is suitable for small pieces, particularly jewellery; however number 1 is a more useful size. If you want to create larger pieces a 2 is better as the bigger base plate allows you to make larger formers.

Before buying a fly-press it is important to consider that you have a space large enough for the press to be operated safely. There must be space for the arm to rotate and the operator to be able to stand far enough away not to be at risk of being struck by the arm as it moves around the central column. It should also not be positioned where a passer-by could accidentally stray into its path.

When setting up the press it should be placed on a heavy-duty stand that is strong enough to take the weight of the press. The press should be safely screwed into the stand and then the stand screwed into the floor. It is very important that the press and stand are secured so there is no movement.

EXERCISE

Making a Vase

EQUIPMENT

- Former – MDF minimum 2.5cm depth
- Set square
- Scroll saw/coping saw
- Drill 2mm
- Wood file
- Pewter disc, diameter 11cm and 0.7mm gauge
- Piercing saw
- Flat metal file
- Emery stick, covered in a 400 emery paper
- Permanent pen
- Dividers
- Fly-press
- Vina mould sheet, melted into a flat sheet approx 3cm deep and 15cm x 15cm wide
- Steel or wooden block (wooden block larger than the pattern being stamped, though steel may be less)
- Vice and vice protectors

Making the Former

Cut a square of MDF approximately 16cm square. Mark the centre of the wood on both sides by drawing a cross from corner to corner. Using this as the central point with a set square draw a line running 90 degrees from the base to the top. Use the set square to then create a line running vertically through the centre of the wood on both sides.

Set the compass to 5.5cm to create an 11cm diameter circle and use the marked centre of your wood as the central point; position your dividers and create a circle in the wood. Turn the wood over and repeat the process. Once the form has been cut out of the wood this will be

Cutting out the former ready for stamping.

your guide as to where to position your pewter when it is being pressed. This ensures that the pewter discs are stamped the same both sides, so that when they are being soldered together the pieces fit each other exactly.

Using the vase template at the back of the book, trace the design and transfer it onto a piece of card. Cut out the card and draw round this onto your wood. The template is designed to extend beyond the drawn circle. Line up the dotted line on the template with the circle drawn on the wood. This allows the top of the vase to flare out, creating the opening for the flowers to go in, when the two pieces are soldered together. If this extended piece is not added to your pattern, the top part of the circle will catch on the wood when being pressed and create a messy line at the top of the vase instead of a flowing one.

Once your design is marked out drill a hole large enough to fit your scroll saw blade through on the inside of your line. If you are not experienced with the saw keep the blade on the inside of the line, as you can use a file to remove any excess and create a smooth line without any lumps after your shape has been cut out. If you do use a file to neaten up the line, keep your file at a 90-degree angle to the wood, as if you file a sharp angle into the wood, when you press the two halves together the stamped pattern will be slightly larger on one of the sides. This will not be too obvious, until you look on the inside of the vase when it is soldered together or look at the vase in profile. It is because of this problem of getting a 90-degree angle that it is not recommended to use a coping saw, as unless you are an experienced wood worker it is very difficult to maintain the correct angle.

Preparing the Metal

You can buy pre-cut pewter discs, and if you are looking to create multiples it is a good idea to do so; however if not, use your dividers still set at 5.5cm to mark out two circles close to the edge of your sheet so you are not wasting pewter. Following the line cut out the circle using a piercing saw. Once complete neaten up the edges with a file, followed by the emery stick to remove file marks and burrs created by the saw and file. Take a permanent pen take your pen and a ruler and draw a line down the centre of your circle from top to bottom, using the mark created by the dividers as a central point. (It is important not to use a scriber or anything that will mark the metal permanently as this will mean a lot more finishing when the piece is ready to be polished.)

Setting up the Fly-Press

Raise the arm of the press by twisting it in an upward direction. If you can secure the arm with rope or something similar to a hook in the wall it will free one hand to set up the work beneath. Place your former on the base of the press under the central column and then position the pewter disc on top of the former within the marked circle, lining up the line on the pewter disc and the line on the wood (shown here as a dotted line).

Place the Vina mould sheet on top of the pewter being careful not to move the pewter below, place the wood then steel sheet on top. The wood is to prevent the steel cutting into the rubber and evenly distributes the weight. It is possible to just use wood, as long as it is a hard wood and is thick enough not to buckle and crack under the pressure of the fly-press when it is released. Before attempting to press the pewter check that when the arm

Press ready to stamp: steel block, wood, vinamould and former.

Stamped-out shape.

is released it does come into contact with the former; sometimes if using a thin former it is not high enough for the central column to reach it. If this is the case another block of wood may need to be placed underneath to raise the height.

When everything is lined up and the former is at the correct height, rotate the arm around the column raising the central plate; before releasing the arm ensure there is no one in the area that may be injured by the handle of the press. When you are confident it is safe to release, swing the arm round then assert some pressure by pushing into the arm to force the rubber into the former. Too much pressure will cut the shape out rather than leaving the disc whole.

Once you have pressed the piece twist the arm back up into a safe position and secure, lift off the blocks and rubber. You should now be able to see that the pewter has been forced down into the former. If you feel you would like the recess to be deeper it is possible to repeat the process, but be aware of not going too far and cutting the pewter.

When the shape is pressed the pewter is drawn into the former; it can make the edge of the disc flare slightly in an upward direction. The two halves need to be completely flat for when they are soldered together, so if this happens put the pewter back in the wooden former and place just the wood and steel block on top, not the Vina mould; make sure it is covering the whole of the disc, then release the arm. This flattens the edge back down onto the edge of the wooden former below, creating a flat back ready for soldering. Make sure the wood covers the whole of the pewter, as if it is only partially covered when the arm is released it will stamp a line into the disc and it is very difficult to remove this completely.

To make the second half of the vase turn the wooden former over and repeat the whole process. You should then finish with two halves that line up perfectly when put together.

Making the Feet

Along the line running down the centre of the disc make a mark with a pen 1cm up the line from what will be the base of the vase. A line now needs to be drawn across the bottom of the disc to mark were it will be bent to make one half of the foot. The vertical line is only used to mark the 1cm mark from the base of the circle; the horizontal line will have to be marked by eye. As the pewter is

Folding the feet.

pressed it moves and stretches within the former so the vertical line will no longer sit centrally. You will need to look at where the vase flares, as this will need to be at the top, and then you will need to draw the horizontal line at the base for a guide to bend the foot. When looking at the line check that it runs parallel to the opening at the top. If it does not and one side is lower than the other when it is filled with water it will pour out of the lower side. It can be lower and not be a problem, and this can sometimes be an interesting design feature, it is just as this is a small vase it reduces the amount of water that can be put in it.

To ensure the foot is in the same position on the second half, hold the two halves together in the position they will be when soldered; then using a permanent pen take the line on the first half round to the front of the second half making two marks either side, then using a ruler join the two marks together. You should now find when the two halves are put together, the line for the foot flows neatly around both sides.

Place the protectors over the jaws of the vice. For a neat folded line the protectors need to be undamaged, or alternatively it is possible to use two pieces of wood instead and sandwich the pewter between them. Position and secure the first half in the vice with the jaws lined up with the line you have drawn. Make sure the hollowed out part of the disc is facing away from you and the raised section is towards you or the foot will be bent in the wrong direction. Once it is positioned correctly hold a piece of wood

behind the disc so you get an even pressure and fold the vase towards you to a 90-degree angle. You can then release the vice and repeat the process with the second half of the vase.

Soldering Together

The two halves are now ready to be soldered together. Before soldering using a fine steel wool rub across the inside of both halves ensuring you go in one direction only. This not only creates a grease-free surface for the soldering but gives the inside of the vase a matt finish.

Note: If you would like the inside of the vase to be polished, at this stage polish the section that will be on show when soldered together, as is will be too difficult once the piece has been soldered. After you have polished the inner section it is still important to wire wool around the edge of the inside surface to remove any grease so the solder can flow freely.

Hold the two halves together with binding wire in two directions to create an even pressure. Flux the two halves, trying not to let too much run over the surface of the vase but keeping it within the joint, as flux on the surface can encourage the solder to flow into it, which means more cleaning. Position the vase on a firebrick; you may need to build other bricks around it to make it stable while soldering.

It is easier to use the stick soldering method on this piece, as there are larger surface areas and the solder will

Soldering the two halves together.

be drawn in. It is easier to feed the stick in, rather than stopping and starting cutting little pieces of solder. There may be a slightly larger gap at the base; more solder can be fed into this area to ensure there are no gaps.

Finishing

Once the two halves are soldered together rinse off the flux and dry. File the two edges either side of the foot, using the metal file. File the surface away so you can no longer see the joint. When you have filed all round the edges go over them with the emery stick removing the file marks and burrs so it is ready to go onto the polisher.

It is difficult to solder the edge as it is a thin area. If any solder does go onto the surface of the vase, avoid using a file. If a lump of solder has built up in one place the easiest way to remove it is to gently heat the solder; when molten using the side of your tweezers slide it across the solder away from the vase so removing the solder. It may be necessary to do this a couple of times; care should be taken not to melt the pewter. The excess can then be removed with emery paper 400, then 600 grade; if a small piece of emery is wrapped around a flat needle file and rubbed just

over the area it is possible to remove it without affecting the surrounding areas. You should be careful not to cause excessive marking on the surface as it can create a lot more work. Avoid using the emery paper with just your finger; this may be tempting but as your finger is soft it will remove the area around the solder as well, whereas if you use a file, as it is hard it will only remove the raised areas.

Before moving on to finishing the vase fill it with water to make sure there are no holes; it is better to do this before polishing as sometimes the polishing compound can fill a hole so it will not become apparent until it has been used several times and the polish has been washed away.

The vase is now ready to be polished (*see* Chapter 6). Try to polish in one direction, not forgetting to do under the foot and the edges. Once completed it may be necessary to use the wire wool again on the inside to remove any marks left by the flux.

Position the vase on a flat surface so you can make sure it is still vertical. Sometimes the pressure of the polisher may force it slightly to one side. As the pewter is soft this can be easily adjusted with your hands.

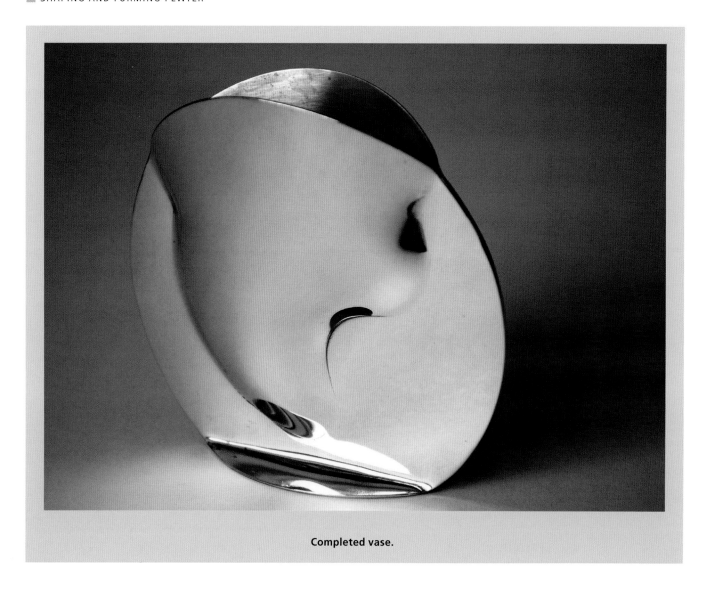

Completed vase.

If you want to create a batch production of certain items, it is possible to get quite a few from an MDF former. However over time the edges start to become rounded so it can lose its definition. To avoid this you can make a Perspex former which can last a lot longer. It is possible to get several hundred pressings from one Perspex former as long as it is used carefully and thicker Perspex is used.

Alternative Pressing Techniques

There are many variations for using the press. One half can be stamped out and then soldered onto a flat sheet, as on this pewter and walnut box. Once the pressed form had been soldered onto the flat sheet the castings were then soldered onto the top of the box.

It is possible to make larger pieces; a thicker gauge of pewter sheet is needed to give the piece more strength. For these larger pieces the Vina mould may not have enough resist to stamp the pewter into the former, so it may be easier to use a heavy-duty rubber, the kind that is used in commercial rubber matting. Cut it into shape slightly smaller than that of the former and allow for the thickness of the metal.

When using this rubber it is necessary to round the edges with a file or emery paper as it is quite hard, and if left in its cut state it will create an angled edge on the pressing. If using thicker gauge pewter like 2mm for stamping,

Pewter and walnut box, author.

immersing the pewter into a bowl of boiling water for a couple of minutes will soften the metal and make it more pliable for stamping.

Building up layers of the rubber, again rounding the edges so it does not create steps, can make a deeper pressing.

Placing a softer rubber, the kind that is used for computer mouse mats, over the top of the layers can stop the hard layers marking the pewter, creating ridges. With thick pewter more pressure is required when swinging the arm of the press to increase the depth.

Seaweed on a Beach (2), carved walnut and pewter, author (photographer Steve Speller).

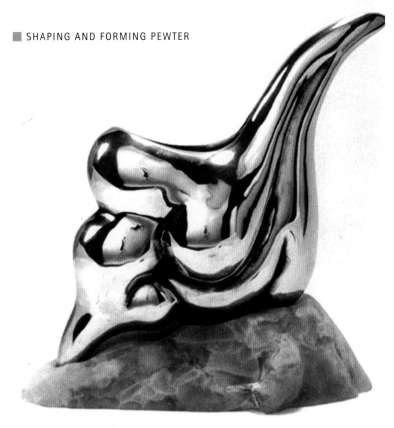

Pewter and cast glass vase, two halves stamped then soldered together, author.

To create the hollowed section on Sea Weed on a Beach sculpture (2), once the desired depth was reached, the hollowed section was filled with clay, then turned upside down so the flat side was on the worktop. It was then clamped to the surface to restrict movement while being worked on. The pewter was hammered down with an embossing mallet in the areas that I wanted to be concave, and the clay acted as a resist, giving the pewter support. To finish, the whole piece was initially polished. The area around the carved wood section was blackened, then with pumice and a brush some of the black areas were pumiced away. This was to create a contrast between the wood and the pewter on the high and low points.

This method can be good for creating details in the piece, as done on the Pewter and Cast Glass Vase, because there is a former. I removed the clay, put the pewter back into the former and using various shaped mallets, hammered certain sections deeper. This way, similarly to *repoussé* techniques, you can work the pewter from both sides.

When making a former for a stamping, avoid small tight curves, as it is difficult using the Vina mould sheet to pick up these details. If making small pieces this sort of curve can be achieved by making a different type of former, like the one shown, where there is a positive part to your former. This can also be produced in wood but again Perspex will last longer.

When making objects like the vase, where the actual stamping is cut out, as well as flattening the piece on the press, it can also be hammered. Place each half separately onto a steel plate, then using a piece of wood and a hammer, keeping the wood as close to the outside line of the stamped shape as possible, hammer all around the shape with each blow slightly overlapping the other. This will ensure the edge of the stamped piece will be flat all the way round. When the shape is cut out the piece is rubbed over a coarse emery paper on the flat plate to give an even flat edge. The two halves can be matched exactly and when soldered will create a neat joint all the way round.

When creating a former, whether it is in wood or Perspex, consider the depth you would like to press. The former will need to be thicker than the desired depth or it will hit the base plate and create a flat front to your design. The salt and pepper shown were made by **Nobuko Okurmura** using a Bonny Doon press. These elegant salt and peppers were inspired by tailor's chalk – the shape, how it fits perfectly in your hand and how it is used. All of these elements were adapted to create an ergonomic, practical salt and pepper cruet. They were made on a Bonnie Doon press, which is similar to a fly-press except it uses hydraulic pressure rather than being manually operated and therefore more intricate shapes can be produced.

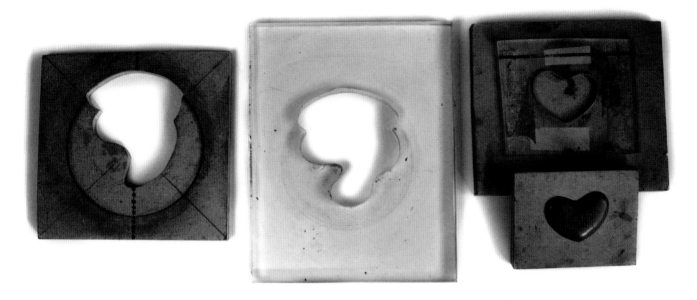

Various types of formers made in wood and Perspex.

Tailor's Salt and Pepper, Nobuko Okumura.

CHAPTER 6

POLISHING AND FINISHING

Bird of Paradise set: cheese knife and cake server, author.

Polishing and finishing pewter is a very important part of creating a pewter piece. It can also be the most time consuming. It is however time well spent as a badly polished piece can ruin the overall look when it is finished.

Many people associate pewter with the traditional dull grey finish, and they are still surprised by the highly polished lustre similar to silver that is achieved with the pewter used today.

Many metalworkers find polishing pewter more difficult than polishing other metals; while this may be true, it is a skill that once practised can produce a high lustre finish to each piece.

There are two basic methods of polishing, firstly using a bench polisher and secondly using a barrel polisher. Both produce a highly polished finish, but it is important to ascertain which finish will be more appropriate. A small delicate design will be better suited to a barrel polisher, as a bench

OPPOSITE PAGE:
Bird of Paradise serviette rings by the author.

polisher may be too aggressive. On the flip side of this a simple design with large flat areas of polished pewter will attain a better finish if it is done on a bench polisher. The size of the finished piece often determines which polisher is appropriate, as the barrel polisher is limited by the size of the barrel as to whether it may be used or not. You can buy larger industrial barrel polishers, but these are not necessarily appropriate for a small workshop.

Bench Polisher

The bench polisher is predominantly used for larger pieces of pewter work. You can buy either a double ended or a single spindle motor, and these come in various sizes from 0.5hp (horse power) up to the more industrial machines of 5hp. For most workshops a 0.5hp will be suitable, but if you tend to work on a larger scale you may find a 1hp better.

Bench polisher.

When setting up your polishing motor you should consider that the process can create a lot of dust so if you do have an area that can be separated from the rest of the workshop it is better. Some polishing motors come with built-in extraction units, however if yours does not, fine dust extractors can be bought quite cheaply. However if you are not going to be polishing for long periods of time a vacuum cleaner with a hose can be used if the hose is connected below the mop and a simple wooden hood placed over the mop, this will stop a lot of the dust being circulated around the room.

For your safety when working with a bench polisher, always wear goggles or a full face mask. Do not wear any loose clothing, and always ensure long hair is tied up so it cannot get caught on the mops when they are rotating.

When holding work against the polishing mop always keep the work below the middle of the front of the mop. If you take it above this line the work can be snatched from your hands.

Try to get in the habit of not standing directly in front of the wheel, so if the item being polished does get caught you are not in its direct path. Because of the movement of the mop the item rarely gets thrown directly towards the operator, but rather usually up or to the back. To be on the safe side stand to the side of the wheel to minimize any risks.

Never walk away and leave the motor switched on. You or someone else may go to use it and not realize it is already on.

Preparing the Piece

Before finishing your piece on the polisher, you must prepare the pewter by cleaning up joints and removing excess solder, hammer marks and scratches. There are many pieces of equipment that will assist in this, including:

Files: Files are the starting point when cleaning up a piece, whether it has been cut or soldered. A set of good general files will contain a flat, half round and oval. You will also need a wire brush; due to the pewter being soft it can clog files quite quickly. If it can be avoided try not to use the file on the surface of your designs. Ideally you just want to use files to clean up soldered joints; as the pewter is soft it takes a lot more work to remove file marks. Files come in various cuts ranging from 00 (very rough) to 4 (very fine). A No.2 is a good general purpose file; some of the very fine files are quite difficult to use with pewter because they become clogged too quickly.

Needle files: Ideal for cleaning small intricate areas.

Riffler files: Double-ended curved and shaped files ideal for difficult areas.

Emery stick: Length of wood with a sheet of emery paper wrapped round it, so as it gets worn away, fresh emery paper can be unwrapped and used. Made from a length of wood approximately 30cm length x 2.5cm width x 1cm depth. Wrap a whole sheet of emery paper tightly around the stick, then hold the ends in place with a masking tape. 400 grit is a good general grade of paper, with 220 when a coarser grade is needed or 600 for finer.

Hand blocks: Rubber bonded abrasive blocks, which come in various grades 60,120 and 240. The advantage of these blocks is that they can be easily cut and shaped, so if there is a particular section of a piece that is difficult to clean with a file, these blocks can be shaped to exactly what you need.

Polishing compounds, wire brush, scotch mop, polishing mops, stitched and unstitched, abrasive rubber blocks and water of Ayr stone.

Rubber abrasive wheels: Made of the same material as the hand blocks but made to fit onto a polishing motor so they are ideal when wanting to clean larger areas.

Water of Ayr stone: A natural stone found in Scotland. Ideal for cleaning file marks from difficult-to-reach places or intricate details. As the stone is hard it can be filed to quite small or intricate shapes, but unlike the rubber it will not distort. It should be used with water and it removes the minimal amount of metal. Once the area has been cleaned it should be washed to remove any stone dust before going onto the polisher.

Abrasive compound: A greaseless compound for applying direct to a polishing mop. It is a mixture of an abrasive and glue. This compound can remove the pewter quickly, so extreme care should be taken if using this.

All of the products listed above can be used to prepare the pewter for the polisher. It is possible to go straight to the polisher from 400 emery, but the piece is a larger flat area it is better to go to a 600. Once you have emeryed the piece and removed all file marks it is ready to go onto the polisher.

Polishing Mops

There are a wide variety of mops available whether it is for a specific part of the polishing process or a specific object such as the inside of a tube. It is advisable to build up a selection of them as certain jobs may require a particular size of mop. The main ones used with the pewter are an open calico mop for the preliminary polishing and a swansdown for the final buffing.

Open calico mop: A good general mop for using with the Hyfin or Tripoli. It is made from whole discs of fabric with a leather washer stapling it all together in the middle. As it is an open mop it has flexibility for polishing round a piece and getting into corners and curves.

Stitched mop: Made from whole discs of fabric but with stitched circles radiating from the centre, which give the mop more strength. These are for the initial polishing as they can be more aggressive. It is possible to retain the strength of the stitched mop but create a softer edge by cutting and removing the outer row of stitches. This is better for large flat areas as it has the stability but is also not too hard for the pewter.

Felt mop: Can be shaped to fit specific jobs. Extreme care should be applied if using it on pewter, as the pewter is so soft the felt mop can cut it, creating grooves in the surface which are very difficult if not impossible to remove.

Swansdown mop: A very soft cotton mop to be used with the rouge. It is an open mop and is always used for the final polishing process.

You will need to select the mop for the type of job you are doing. It is a good idea to try them out with the various polishing compounds, to see which is most suitable.

Polishing Compound

The polishing compound is the abrasive that is applied to the mop to complete the polishing processes. A commercial manufacturer will do most of the work on the polisher, missing out the emery paper process. Under each polisher they have a tray with a combination of oil and pumice which at regular intervals is thrown against the mop and as it is so abrasive it removes the surface on the pewter. This is ideal for a large-scale manufacturer as hundreds of items are needed to be cleaned quickly and there is the space to create a separate working area for this process. It is a messy process and needs to be contained in a separate area.

Most small workshops would not be equipped to do this, so working through the various hand finishing processes is more practical. The main polishing compounds for pewter are:

Tripoli: A slightly more abrasive compound typically used on most other base metals like brass and copper and also on precious metals such as silver and gold. This works well with the pewter if there is need for more initial cleaning. It is known as a cutting compound. This can be used with the stitched mops or the open mops.

Hyfin: A dry finishing compound used by many jewellers and silversmiths as it is less abrasive and not greasy like the Tripoli. It can be used with the stitched mops or the open mops.

Rouge: For a mirror-like finish rouge is the traditional buffing compound. Again it is a dry compound and there are various types and grades available. It is used with a swansdown mop and should be used as part of the final process when finishing a piece.

Menzerna yellow super finish: An alternative to rouge, it is a dry polishing compound so does not leave the compound on the piece as the rouge quite often does. When used with a soft swansdown mop it produces an excellent mirror-like finish.

Starting to Polish

When using a new mop the mop will need to be 'dressed'. This removes any loose threads; it also ensures the mop is running true and causes the surface threads to knit together making a soft surface on the mop. Loose threads will drag on the pewter and create lines on the surface as you polish. Some mops are now pre-dressed when you buy them. It is however very simple: place the mop on the spindle. Do not screw it all the way on allow but the machine to take the mop; you may screw it on unevenly whereas the machine will not.

The wheel will need to be dressed. This is done using a rake specifically designed for the process: a stiff brush or, alternatively, nails hammered through a piece of wood. Turn the motor on and slowly move the rake from side to side across the wheel. This will create a lot of dust so make sure your clothing is covered and you are wearing a mask. Once the mop is dressed it is ready for the polishing compound to be applied.

Sometimes a mop will become dirty if has not been used for a while, or alternatively if it has been used a lot for polishing a hard crust might have built up on the perimeter of the mop. It will need to be cleaned using the same process described for dressing the wheel.

If the piece needs a more abrasive compound start with a Tripoli mop, but if this is not necessary as in most cases a Hyfin-coated mop will be suitable to start with. Once that process has been complete move onto a swansdown with rouge or Menzerna yellow. Try to keep separate mops for each compound; labelling the side with a marker pen is often a good idea.

Once the mop has been dressed/cleaned turn the motor on and, using the correct compound for the mop and process you are doing, gently hold it against the mop while it is rotating, moving the block side to side across the block. Hold it for a couple of rotations of the mop; this should be enough.

Polishing (photographer Wilf Speller).

Working on a small polisher you may find you prefer to wear gloves, as the pewter can become quite hot. If working on an industrial polisher there is a danger of the glove becoming caught in the mop and pulling in the operator's hand, so gloves cannot be worn.

The mop rotates in a downward direction. For this reason when polishing the object should always be positioned below the halfway line of the front of the mop. If it is put onto the mop above this point the polisher can snatch the piece out of your hand. Because of the movement of the mop if this does happen it is more likely the object will be thrown away from the operator, but if it hits any objects nearby it can create dents and scratches in the piece.

Try to polish in one direction. If working on a larger piece, do not attempt to polish the whole piece from one side as it is difficult to see what is happening and also it can become caught on the mop. Turn the whole piece round and start again from the opposite direction.

When swapping the mops and using a different compound polish in a different direction to the previous process. Even if the angle is just slightly different it will affect the finish. If

constantly going in one direction the mops creates very small grooves; these will become deeper and this will affect the final surface finish. However if the piece is being moved in a different direction it will remove the high points, keeping the surface flat.

When polishing a straight edge move the piece in a downward, sweeping movement across the mop at an angle; if it is polished straight up and down it will create grooves in the mop which will affect the surfaces of any further polished work. Also if the piece is polished horizontally to the mop this will act like a scraper removing all the compound.

Very little pressure is needed while polishing, just a firm grip to hold onto the piece. With the smaller polishers too much pressure on the mop will stop it from rotating. It is important to keep the piece moving so the mop does not start to cut into the metal and create deep impressions in the surface.

Once the piece has been completely finished it can be washed with warm soapy water, drying immediately afterwards with a soft cloth to remove any dirt or grease left on the surface.

PROBLEMS

Small scratches visible on the surface? This could be caused by file marks and saw marks that were not thoroughly removed. Reuse the emery, then repeat the polishing process.

Small pitted holes in the surface? If the piece is a casting and small pitted holes appear as it is polished, it may be a bad casting. They may be removed with a file, then by emerying again, but sometimes filing can just expose more holes. If using sheet, the holes may be caused by tiny air pockets created in the pewter when it was rolled into sheet; again, poor quality metal.

Polishing compound smears on the surface? This can sometimes be caused if the polishing mop becomes overloaded with the compound. Clean the mop by running the rake or stiff brush over the mop surface while it is rotating to remove some of the excess compound. Remove the compound from the metal, then polish over it with the cleaned mop in the opposite direction, and this will remove the smear.

Do not keep polishing over the top of the residue compound without cleaning the mop. The metal will be removed from around the smear, so that when the piece is cleaned up there will be a raised section were the compound had adhered to the surface, creating a rippled effect on the pewter.

Barrel Polisher

A barrel polisher is used as an alternative to the bench polisher giving the pewter a highly polished bright finish. It uses the same principles as a stone tumbler, which you may have seen or used at some time. A plastic or rubber barrel is placed on two spindles which are then rotated by a small motor. The contents are spun in a small amount of water and barrel polishing compound; the compound helps to lubricate the steel shot and the work and also helps to keep the steel shot in good condition. As a result the surface of the contents is burnished to create a polished finish.

The barrel polisher is ideal for polishing small pieces or parts, particularly those with a lot of detail that could possibly be removed if bench polishing mops were used. It is more economical if time is a consideration on a piece as several pieces can be put into a barrel at a time and it is then left, unlike having to give your time and attention to hand polishing.

The metal barrel polishers can have either one or two plastic or rubber barrels rotating at the same time. Steel shot, which is made up of various shapes and sizes, is placed inside the barrel. As the barrel rotates the steel shot will bounce over the

Barrel polisher.

surface of the pieces slowly burnishing it and creating a highly polished finish. The shot comes in various shapes such as round balls, pins, diagonally cut cylinder pieces and diamond shapes. Each is designed to account for the variety of contours on a piece, so no areas will be left unpolished.

The shot is placed in the barrel with water and a barrel polishing compound (this helps to lubricate the shot and polish the work). The work is then also placed inside. Follow guidelines for the machine that you will be using regarding the weight of the work put in. If it is too heavy the barrel will not rotate and it will strain the motor.

A cast piece can be put directly into the polisher without having to do very much work, only removing the sprue and any flashing that may have occurred around the piece (this can be simply removed by scraping it off with a knife). If pieces have had to be worked on prior to going into the polisher, for example pieces soldered together or if the sprue is quite large and needs to be cut with a saw, remove any rough areas with a file and then finish with a piece of 400 emery paper. The piece is then ready to be put into the polisher.

The amount of time the piece is in the polisher can vary from 20 minutes upwards, depending upon the size and shape of the piece. Just keep checking the pieces at regular intervals until they are completely polished. To remove the pieces empty the contents into a sieve placed over a bowl. Then remove the pieces, rinse them thoroughly and then dry them.

It is possible to reuse the solution several times, but if it becomes too dirty it must be changed. When changing it empty the shot into the sieve, then rinse the barrel before adding the new solution.

To ensure the steel shot does not become rusty do not leave it without any solution. If it does for any reason become slightly rusty place the shot in the barrel with solution and turn the machine on and the shot will then burnish itself. It may take several attempts and you will need to change the solution between each attempt. This will however only work for very mild cases of rust. If it has gone too far and the surface of the shot has become pitted it will no longer be suitable as the pitted marks will just scratch the surface of the work.

If the tumbler is also used for polishing silver it is better to have a separate barrel and shot for the pewter to reduce any risk of contamination.

Mini Fungi spirit levels, author

Oak Leaf serviette rings, Glover and Smith.

Creating a Matt Finish

It may be that a polished finish is not appropriate for some designs and matt finish is more suitable.

To use a barrel polisher to give pieces a matt finish, ceramic chips are placed in the barrel instead of the steel shot. These chips are usually cone shaped and can come in various grades, some being quite coarse. With a cutting compound they can be used instead of an emery paper to remove scratches. Care should be taken if using these on detailed pieces as some of the finer lines can be removed.

There are several other ways to create a matt finish: sandblasting, pumice powder, satin mop or wire wool.

Sandblasting: This creates an even matt surface. Sand is forcefully thrown against the piece at high pressure in an enclosed chamber. This process can be used to take away more of the surface, so it does not necessarily need to be polished beforehand. Patterns can be created by marking off areas with tape on the whole piece and cutting out certain sections so that there is a pattern with a polished and matt contrast.

Note: Before using any of these other finishes the piece does still need to be polished; this ensures that there are no scratches. As the techniques to make the surface matt are so fine, any other scratches left by a file or a saw would be too deep and would still be obvious on the surface.

Pumice powder: Very finely ground pumice is mixed with a small amount of water to make a thick paste. Then using a toothbrush rub the powder over the surface, rinsing at intervals to check there is an even finish. It may be necessary to go over the surface several times to produce a good matt finish. Patterns can be created as in the sandblasting process by marking off areas to create contrasts of polished and matt surface. If doing this make sure the edge of the tape is securely stuck to the surface or the line will become blurred.

Satin mops: Used on a bench polisher or much smaller size can be used on a pendant drill. Made of built-up layers of woven fibre very similar to kitchen scourers. Each layer is approximately 5mm thick and is impregnated with aluminium oxide that creates an abrasive finish. They come in various widths and diameters. The bench polishing mops make it easier to give larger pieces a satin finish and come in various grades: very fine, fine, medium and coarse. The mop should be moved on the polisher so that *the pattern is going in one direction*.

Wire wool: Fine wire wool if rubbed across the surface in one direction can also create a matt finish.

Looking after Pewter

It takes very little maintenance to keep pewter clean. As a general rule pewter should be cleaned every once in a while with soapy water and a soft cloth, then dried immediately so that water marks are not left on the surface. Do not use an abrasive scourer, particularly on a polished finish, as it will scratch the surface. Pewter should never be cleaned in a dishwasher.

Obviously when a piece is fresh off the polisher it will have a particularly highly polished finish. With just general daily use and being in the air this will start to fade a bit, but certainly not to the same level as other metals such as silver, brass and copper, all of which build up an oxide layer that completely changes the appearance of the metal if a cleaning regime is not maintained.

If the pewter needs a little more than soap and water it is possible to use a fine silver cleaner. Ensure you apply it in one direction only, and make sure the cleaner is for silver, as some other metal cleaners can be too abrasive for pewter. Once cleaned, wash with hot soapy water and dry it straight away with a soft cloth. This will remove any residue left by the polish.

If you have an old piece of pewter, metal cleaner is not recommended. Only soapy water should be used.

Fish skeleton found on the beach.

CHAPTER 7

DESIGN AND THE FUTURE OF PEWTER

Design

When people think about design many do not realize what a huge area it is and how our lives are affected by it on a daily basis. We are constantly surrounded by 'things' that someone has designed whether it is as functional as a chair or a pen or decorative like a picture or a sculpture. People now expect good design for general everyday objects.

The challenge as a maker is to keep striving to develop and make new pieces. Producing the same things over and over again can become boring. Creating new ideas makes it stimulating and interesting not only for the craftsperson but for the people who see the work as well. If your work is constantly changing people will be intrigued to see how it is developing. Challenging yourself with new ideas and techniques stimulates enthusiasm for your work.

Inspiration

People are inspired by so many things: nature – plants, insects, shells…; architecture – bridges, churches, houses…; transport – planes, cars, trains…; design movements – Art Nouveau,

Dandelion seeds.

Damsel fly.

Dried-up mud left by a puddle of rain.

Detail inside the *Sagrada Familia*, Gaudi, Barcelona.

Arts and Crafts, Art Deco, Bauhaus...; History – Egyptians, Romans, Victorians...; visits to museums and art galleries ... the list can go on and on.

It is not only the objects that can inspire a piece; a technical process can develop into a whole series of work. An example of a technical process inspiring work is laser cutting. A few years ago when it became readily accessible, suddenly high street shops had lots of products made using the laser-cutting process; fine intricate lampshades, decorative bowls and other everyday objects were being produced on a large scale, having filtered down to large-scale manufacturers from individual designers who had initially developed ideas and explored its possibilities.

If designing and developing ideas is an area that is new to you it can help to keep a sketch book where you can stick images that you find interesting or make quick drawings. Today many of us carry a mobile phone that has a camera; this means we can take pictures anywhere, it might be that just walking to work we see an interesting flower or reflection in some water. Be aware of what is around you, not necessarily looking at the whole shape – it may be just a small detail: a tail light on a vintage car, the wing of a dragonfly. It could also be as simple as just a line: the line of a ballet dancer's arm, the wing of a bird in flight or the skyline of a town or city.

You may choose a historical event, such as the 1066 Battle of Hastings, or investigate a new culture with its customs,

Lacewing nest on a banana leaf, inspiration for sculpture.

ceremonies or costumes. It does not have to be a physical object that you can see or touch; it may be an emotion or a feeling. By becoming more aware of your environment, researching and looking at things in a different way, you can start to collect pieces that will inspire you.

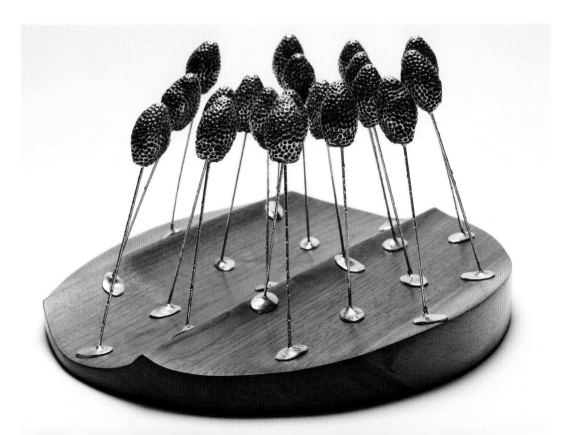

Lacewing Nest Sculpture, carved walnut and pewter, author (photographer Steve Speller).

Design Development

If you were to ask several makers how they develop ideas you are likely to get many different answers. Everybody works differently. Some people develop ideas through drawings and then make models; others may produce some quick sketches and then start to make models; and similarly some may make a quick sketch and then develop an idea as they work on the actual piece; or as discussed earlier a technical process may be a starting point. There is no right or wrong way; it is just a matter of finding a way that you prefer to work.

For me if working with a new source I produce large charcoal drawings, playing around with shapes and lines from the inspirational object or image. I then make models usually in clay, wax or plaster. I develop these models to make them more refined and work out any details in a layout pad. As the paper is quite thin if I have a shape that I like but I would like to change a small detail I can turn the page over, draw the shape again and alter the section. I may draw lots of the same thing but draw a detail differently on each one, so I could end up with many pages of the same shape with just small differences before I settle on one design. Then I start to work on the final piece.

Once I have worked out a form and made a piece this usually inspires other pieces to make a collection. An example of this is the design of the serviette rings. After making some quick sketches of a ballet dancer moving, I used some of these drawings and started to work with charcoal, focusing particularly on the line created by the arm and leg of the dancer. I then developed these with more detailed drawings in pencil in my sketch book and made a wax model. This simple shape for the serviette ring then inspired designs for the candlesticks and wine bottle stand to form a whole collection to be used on a dining table.

It is useful to have some working knowledge of the pewter, which is why I would encourage experimenting with various techniques. This allows you to make informed decisions about how a piece can be made. Limited knowledge may mean your final piece does not look like your drawn designs as you did not have the experience necessary to do it.

When starting to develop designs, if you have not done much design before try to explore various ways which move you out of your comfort zone. It might be something as simple as buying a roll of lining paper and some charcoal, pastels, brush and ink and moving along the roll of paper producing very quick sketches. You will find as you work along

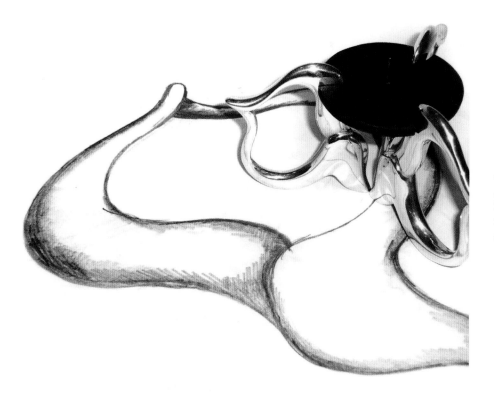

Charcoal drawing and Slate and Pewter Candlestick, inspired by drawing of the movement of a ballerina, author.

Serviette rings, author.

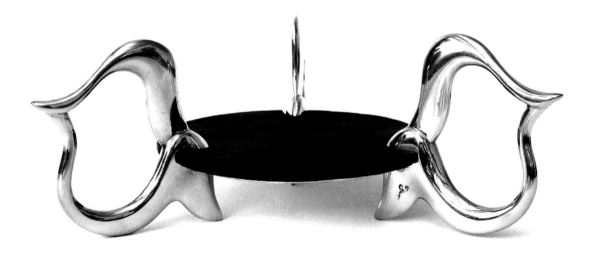

Slate and pewter wine bottle stand, author.

the roll you become more free and looser with the lines and shapes. This can produce some interesting results, and out of all of them it may be that you only find one that you like, but this one could be a starting point.

While studying for my degree we had a day just drawing each week. Very early in the course we were given several pieces of paper and some charcoal, then told to feel the inside of our mouth with our tongue and draw what we felt. Initially it was the most bizarre and difficult thing to do, but then when I started to take it seriously, the more drawings I did the more interesting they become. Feeling the shape and line of my teeth and then transferring it to the paper created some odd and some interesting images. I had never worked in this way before and although initially very uncomfortable with the process, it did make me think more about what I was doing and enabled me to work differently.

Models are a quick way to work out the three-dimensional shape, scale and size of a piece. There are many materials that can be used and quite often it is just what you have to hand – paper or card is often the most accessible – and they can be made quite quickly and held together with tape. They may not look very neat but they can be used to work out a detail quickly that would take twice as long to do if sketched on paper. Keeping some clay can also be useful if trying to work out organic shapes; it can be modelled roughly to size and shape, and then when dried it can be worked into with clay tools and the surface can be made smooth with sandpaper.

Combining Materials

Having chosen to work with pewter does not mean other materials cannot be used. Combining materials can enhance a design, or it can be a practical issue. If wanting to combine pewter with other metals, consideration will need to be given to the fact that they cannot be soldered as the pewter has a much lower melting point than most other metals, so alternative ways of fixing together will need to be used.

I started to do wood carving, as I found certain woods, particularly walnut, work well with the pewter. While creating a series of sculptures based on the beach, I had taken photographs of pebbles on the beach and was particularly interested in how the sea had drawn the sand away from around the pebbles as the tide had gone out. I wanted to make quite a large piece and create a contrast like that of the sand, the pebbles and the shadow around the pebble. The wood worked beautifully as the grain of the wood flowed like the ripples of the sand and I carved it to make the hollow sections for the pebbles to sit in.

The wood also acted as a former. I wanted to make the shadows in pewter, so after cutting the shape out of some pewter sheet I hammered the sheet directly into the hollows in the wood, so the pewter followed the shape perfectly, ready for the pebble to neatly sit on top.

Sometimes a different material will need to be used for practical reasons, such as the glass plate on the Bird of Paradise Cake Stand. If the plate for the cakes had been made

Pebbles on a Beach Sculpture, carved walnut and pewter, author (photographer Steve Speller).

in pewter the constant cutting and scraping with a knife and a server would create quite heavy marking on the surface. Also having a solid surface would have obscured the details of the legs. By using a glass plate for the cakes it can easily be removed and cleaned, and when not in use the intricate detail of the legs is not lost.

The Candlesticks and Wine Bottle Stand combines the pewter with welsh slate. The soft matt grey of the Welsh slate compliments the pewter, and it also makes a practical base for a wine bottle and the candles.

Other craft people also combine pewter with different materials. American designer/craftsman **Jon Michael Route** combines pewter with materials such as brass, copper and aluminium to create a contrast of colour.

Bird of Paradise Cake Stand, author.

Indigenous Teapot,
Jon Michael Route
(photographer Deb Route).

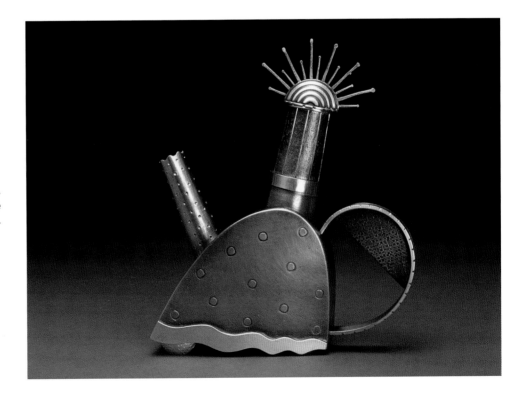

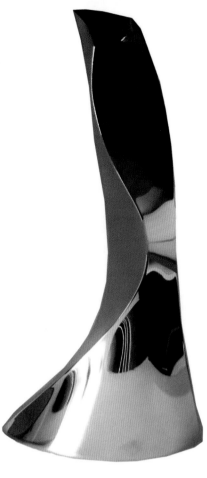

Twisted Vase, designed by Catherine Tutt, produced by A.R. Wentworth (Sheffield) Ltd.

The Future of Pewter

Pewter has for a long time been considered the poor man's silver. It has moved in and out of fashion but has remained in continual use. The long history of pewter and the traditional products made from it, such as tankards and hip flasks, will ensure that pewter continues its presence in people's homes.

However it is no longer just these traditional items that are keeping pewter alive as a creative material. Large pewter manufacturers and individual craftspeople are using it for more contemporary designs and alternative uses; one of the ways that this is being encouraged in the UK is through Pewter Live.

Pewter Live is an annual event organized by The Worshipful Company of Pewterers, with the support of the ABPC the Association of British Pewter Craftsmen. The aim of the event is to revive interest in pewter for domestic and interior products, gifts, jewellery and accessories. Established in 1986, the event maintains a high profile for pewter. It helps to educate people as to what pewter is; there is a demonstration area so people can see pieces being made and witness the various technical processes; the shop shows a wide selection of

pewter products sold; but most importantly it inspires people to design, produce or buy pewter.

Pewter Live hosts a competition to encourage students in their second year of university to work with pewter. There are various categories the students can enter: architectural hardware, decorative arts, fashion; jewellery and accessories. Each university entering the competition is linked with a manufacturer or someone with a working knowledge of pewter to give advice on production, design and techniques. It is an ideal opportunity for the students to work with a company and start to understand production processes and experience the development process for an item that will go into production, as the brief encourages students to consider market requirements and commercial viability.

It is also enlightening for the companies, as they are working with students with great imaginations who are focused on developing new and exciting ideas. As they are still at college they are able to push and explore ideas and techniques perhaps more than a manufacturer or working craftsperson who may not have time due to the economic demands and constraints to be constantly producing work.

Some of these collaborations between students and companies have expanded beyond the competition, with

Garden Flowers, designed by Katy Holford, produced by A.R. Wentworth (Sheffield) Ltd.

certain companies developing the designs, producing them and selling them as part of their range with the student named as the designer. An example of this is The Twisted Vase, designed by **Catherine Tutt** who won first prize in 1996 while studying at Buckinghamshire University. Wentworth was overseeing the project at the university, and following the competition the company put the piece into production and it is now one of the best sellers in its contemporary collection.

In 2005 The Worshipful Company introduced an Open Category for professional designers, manufacturers and designer/makers. Each year a brief is set by the Company to encourage established companies and makers to produce

new ideas and explore alternative areas beyond their usual body of work. This category has also encouraged people who do not normally work with pewter to try using it, as in the case of **Katy Holford** who works as a designer, sculptor and consultant. She designed a range of stylized pewter flower heads, combined with an aluminium top and steel stake. They were designed to support climbing plants and are decorative features within a garden; the designs were produced by Wentworth and are now part of their range.

Pewter is now becoming more recognized. Within the fifteen years I have been working with it there have been a lot of changes. Initially there was a lot of confusion over the colour of pewter, but people now recognize more and more that it is not dull grey. There are a lot more contemporary designs being produced using pewter, and more designers now have a knowledge and understanding of it and its properties. Whether they choose to use it all the time or occasionally it is still raising its profile as a material.

Pewter is now also being used in fresh new ways not normally associated with it. Benchmark Furniture for example incorporates pewter into their designs such as The Silverwing Table, designed by **Terence Conran**. They have also designed and made interiors for hotels, such as the bar and reception area for the My Hotel in Brighton, and the reception desk for 5 Fleet Place in London. All of these are outstanding designs and an innovative use for the pewter.

Parks metals specialize in using pewter as an integral part of interiors for bars and interior fittings. Other interior areas are also being explored such as bathrooms. GNZ Designs are including pewter bathroom fittings and accessories as part of their range. The possibilities for its use are forever expanding. **Caroll Boyes** uses pewter for many functional household items such as the lemon squeezer.

In 2009 when I married there was a pewter theme at the wedding. I made the centrepieces, place card holders, cake knife, favours and tiaras all in pewter, as well as the bouquets for the bride and bridesmaids. As an alternative to the traditional floral bouquet I combined pewter blossom with various types of feather and Swarovski crystal beads, and the buttonholes had a single pewter blossom stem combined with foliage to link with the bouquets.

More schools are now incorporating pewter into projects, as it can be done with a relatively small amount of equipment, pieces can be produced quite quickly and there are no harmful fumes when it is heated, making it suitable for a classroom environment. The fact that pewter is starting to be used more in schools means children are being taught about it at an early age. Who knows, some of these may go on to become pewtersmiths in the future.

Pewter is a material with so many possibilities; it provides pleasure for anyone using it and exploring various ways that it can be used. Today's pewtersmiths may not be the same in number as they were at the height of its popularity, but the skills are still being passed on to stimulate interest in pewter as part of our past, present and future.

The Silverwing Table, designed by Terence Conran, Benchmark.

My Hotel, reception Brighton, Benchmark.

Lemon Squeezer,
Carrol Boyes.

Pewter Bar, Park Metal Construction Ltd (PMC).

**Pewter Plug,
GNZ Designs.**

**Pewter and Swarovski Crystal Bouquet,
author (photographer Steve Speller).**

APPENDIX:
TEMPLATE 1

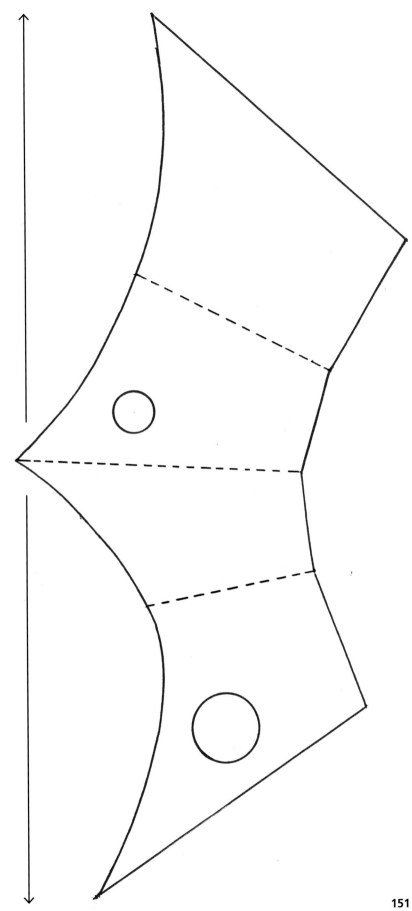

Reduced
from
260mm

Fabricated Vase template.

APPENDIX:
TEMPLATE 2

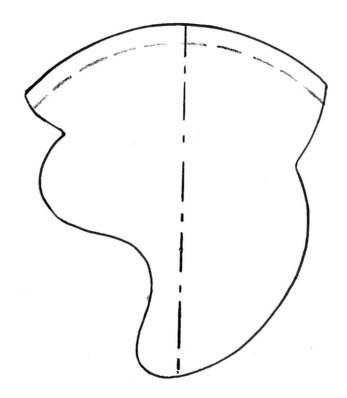

Fly-pressed Vase template.

GLOSSARY

bezel a raised piece of metal that can be pushed over to secure something in place; traditionally used for jewellery to hold stones in place (known as a bezel setting).

blank an object that the pewter is applied to, to give the pewter support and structure, such as boxes, picture frames or jewellery; ready-made blanks can be bought or made.

burr a sharp piece of thin raised metal formed around the edge of a piece of metal that has been filed, cut or emeryed; generally removed so formers and mallets do not become damaged.

Chavant sulphur-free oil-based modelling clay, normally used by sculptors instead of clay as it does not dry out.

cure refers to the process of making liquid rubber solidify by adding a catalyst to cause a chemical reaction; different types of rubber have specific cure periods of time that can be reduced with a booster catalyst, increased temperatures, or in the case of the RTV101 by adding water.

emery stick a length of wood with a sheet of emery paper wrapped round it, so as it gets worn away, fresh emery paper can be unwrapped and used.

flashing extraneous metal left around a casting when the metal spreads beyond the mould cavity and flows in between the two halves of the rubber mould; usually very thin and can be removed with a knife.

former/stake a shape made of steel, nylon, wood etc, used for shaping metal over, on and into, with hammers and mallets.

Hyfin a polishing compound brushed over the surface of the polishing mops used on a bench polisher; usually used for the first stage of polishing.

planishing hammering the surface of the metal onto a stake/former, each strike overlapping to produce a smooth finish and refine the finished shape, using a planishing hammer – a steel hammer with two round ends each having a mirror finish.

resist a material or substance that will not be affected by the acid used to create patterns in the etching process; the acid will only remove the metal where there is no resist.

rouge/jeweller's rouge a polishing compound brushed over the surface of the polishing mops used on a bench polisher; used with a very soft 'swansdown' mop for the final stages of polishing.

scriber a tapered piece of steel which comes to a very fine point, used like a pencil to mark the metal as it produces a shallow cut line.

sprue an extraneous piece of metal produced on a piece being cast when the molten metal in the pouring gate cools and solidifies; this is cut off and can be remelted.

Tripoli a polishing compound brushed over the surface of the polishing mops used on a bench polisher for the first stage of polishing; slightly more abrasive than Hyfin.

undercut a protruding or concave feature of an item being moulded that can cause problems because it can hinder the withdrawal of the cast from the mould; a flexible mould might be pulled over the casting, but a rigid mould can break.

USEFUL ADDRESSES

United Kingdom

FRED ALDOUS LTD
PO Box 135
37 Lever St
Manchester
M60 1UX
www.fredaldous.co.uk
Pewter sheet, repousse tools other modelling materials.

CARN METALS
2c Trewellard Industrial Estate
Pendeen Cornwall TR19 7TF
Telephone: 01736 787343
www.carnmetl.demon.co.uk
Pewter, casting ingots, sheet and solder

COOKSON PRECIOUS METALS
59–83 Vittoria Street
Birmingham,
B1 3NZ
www.cooksongold.com
Machinery, findings and hand tools.

GOLDBRITE LTD
322 Coleford Rd
Sheffield
S9 PH5
Telephone: 0114 2433011
Gold plate pewter.

T.N. LAWRENCE & SON LTD.
208 Portland Road
Hove
BN3 5QT
Tel: 0845 644 3232
www.lawrence.co.uk
Printing suppliers, etching stop out and ferric chloride crystals.

PEWTER SHEET COMPANY LIMITED
River Lee Road
Tyseley
Birmingham
B11 2JG
www.pewtersheet.co.uk
Pewter casting ingot, sheet and discs.

W.H. SAYNOR & SON LTD
Henry St
Sheffield
S3 7EQ
Telephone: 0114 272 9006
Gold plate pewter.

TIRANTI
3 Pipers Court
Berkshire Drive
Thatcham
Berkshire
RG19 4ER
www.tiranti.co.uk
Mould making equipment, model making materials, casting equipment.

THE WORSHIPFUL COMPANY OF PEWTERERS
Pewterers' Hall
Oat Lane
London EC2V 7DE
Telephone: 0207 397 8190
Facsimile: 020 7 600 3896
www.pewterers.org.uk
Email: clerk@pewterers.org.uk

H.S. WALSH & SONS LTD
243 Beckenham Road
Beckenham
Kent
BR3 4TS
www.hswalsh.com
Machinery, findings and handtools.

USA

THE COMPLEAT SCULPTOR
90 Vandam St
New York NY 10013
www.sculpt.com
Modelmaking supplier.

IASCO TESCO
Industrial Arts Supply Co
Technology Education Supply Co
5724 West 36th
Minneapolis
MN55416
Tel: 888-919-0899
www.iasco-tesco.com
Casting equipment.

RIO GRANDE
Albuquerque – NM USA
800-545-6566
www.rio grande.com
Jewellery tools and equipment suppliers.

TEKCAST INDUSTRIES INC
12 Potter Ave
New Rochelle
New York
10801
Free phone 1-800-872 4835
Fax 914-576-007
www.tekcast.com
Pewter supplier.

FURTHER READING

Pewter Working Techniques

Browne. M. *Pewter Jewellery* (B.T. Batsford Ltd, 1979)

Charron. S. *Modern Pewter, Design & Techniques* (David & Charles Holdings Ltd. Publishing UK. Copyright. Litton Educational publishing, Inc. 1973)

Hull, C.J., & Murrel, J.A. *The Techniques of Pewtersmithing.* (B.T. Batsford Ltd, 1984)

Osburn, Burl N., & Wilber, Gordon O *Pewter-working, Instructions and Projects.* (Dover Publications, Inc. 1979)

Mould Making

Sharpe, Martin *Plaster Waste-moulding Casting and Life casting. A manual for the student* (Tiranti Technical Booklet)

The Silicone Rubber Booklet, Cold Cure Silcone Rubber for Mould Making (with a section on low casting alloys) Tiranti Technical Booklet)

Repoussé Techniques

Dundas, Z. *Pewter Relief Modelling (*The Stellar Press. Ltd. 1951)

Griffiths, S. *Pewter Plus* (David & Charles. D&C. 2007)

General

Hedges, E.S. *Tin and its Alloys* (Edward Arnold publishers Ltd. 1960)

Hull, C. *Pewter* (Shire Publications Ltd. 1992)

Smith, K. *Silversmithing – a manual of design and technique* (Crowood Press, 2000)

Untracht, O. *Jewellery Concepts and Technology* (Doubleday & Company, Inc. 1985)

Further Information about Pewter

Pewter Review magazine, The Worshipful Company of Pewterers, Pewterers' Hall, Oat Lane, London, EC2V 7DE.

A.B.P.C. (Association of British Pewter Craftsmen) Unit 10, Edmund Road Business Centre, Sheffield S2 4ED. Tel: 0114 252 7550.

Websites

www.technologystudents.com
www.carnmetl.demon.co.uk
www.ganoksin.com

ACKNOWLEDGEMENTS

I would like to thank my husband and my family for all their constant support, encouragement and patience.

I would also like to say thank you to the many pewterers, designers and craftspeople that gave up their time to help with the book either with their expert knowledge or generously giving me illustrations and descriptions of their work; the Worshipful Company of Pewterers members and staff and the Pewter Industries Charity for their generous support and help collating information; the ABPC (Association of British Pewter Craftsmen) for their guidance and passing on their expert knowledge; A.R. Wentworth (Sheffield) Ltd, in particular Richard and Jayne Abdy, but also all their staff for generously giving up their time to help; the Pewter Sheet Company Ltd, for their expert knowledge producing pewter; and Tony Bryant of Sheffield University, who kindly gave his time to explain various metallurgical facts to help with the author's research,

INDEX